A PROMETHEAN VISION

The Formation of Karl Marx's Worldview

Eric Rahim

'Marx as Prometheus',
tormented by the Prussian censor.
19th century lithograph.

A PROMETHEAN VISION

VISION

The Formation of Karl Marx's Worldview

Eric Rahim

ISBN-13: 978-1-899155-08-8
EAN: 9781899155088

Published by Praxis Press jointly with the Marx Memorial Library
Email: praxispress@me.com
Website: redletterspp.com

Editorial Office: Unity Books, 72 Waterloo Street, Glasgow, G2 7DA,
Scotland, Great Britain
T: +44 141 204 1611
E: enquiries@unitybooks.co.uk
www.unitybooks.co.uk

CONTENTS

CHRONOLOGY (1818-1849)

1818 Born in Trier (5 May), Rhineland, Germany.

1835 Completes high school education.

1835-6 Student of law in Bonn University

1836 Enters Berlin University, studies law, history and philosophy.

1837 Joins the group of Young Hegelians; letter to father informing him on the progress of his studies.

1838 Death of father.

1841 Completes doctoral dissertation on 'Difference Between the Democritean and Epicurean Philosophy of Nature'; graduation at Jena University.

1842 Contributes to and later edits the Cologne newspaper *Rheinische Zeitung (RZ)*.

1843 Resigns from *RZ*; gets married to Jenny von Westphalen; writes 130-page *Contribution to the Critique of Hegel's Philosophy of Law [Right]* (the *Hegel Critique*) not published) and the article 'On the Jewish Question'; moves to Paris (October).

1844 Co-edits (with Arnold Ruge) the journal *Deutsch-Französische Jahrbücher (DFJ)*; publishes 'On the Jewish Question' and 'Introduction' to the *Hegel Critique* in *DFJ*; publishes article 'Critical Notes on 'The King of Prussia and Social Reform'' in the journal *Vorwärts!*; studies French socialism and communism, history of the French Revolution and political economy; first meeting with Frederick Engels, beginning of their friendship and collaboration; writes *The Economic and Philosophical Manuscripts* (not published), and *The Holy Family*.

1845 Expelled from Paris; moves to Brussels (February); writes *Theses on Feuerbach* (not published), adopting his own philosophical standpoint; six-week visit to England, studies political economy in Manchester; with Engels establishes contacts with Chartists and English socialists.

1846   Sets up Communist Correspondence Committee; completes (with Engels) the two-volume *The German Ideology* (not published), presenting for the first time a systematic statement of the materialist conception; letter to P. V. Annenkov (28 December) giving a succinct statement of the materialist conception.

1847   Joins the Communist League; publishes *The Poverty of Philosophy*, the first *published* statement of the materialist conception; lectures on Free Trade, and Wage Labour and Capital; attends congress of the Communist League in London and with Engels is instructed by the congress to draft a manifesto for the League.

1848   *The Communist Manifesto* (written with Engels) published; (revolutionary uprisings in Paris, Vienna and parts of Germany.) Expelled from Brussels; moves to Paris and then to Cologne; establishes a newspaper, *Neue Rheinische Zeitung*; writes numerous commentaries on the revolutions.

1849   After the failure of the uprisings moves to Paris (May); expelled from Paris; moves to London (August).

Introduction

This book is an exposition of Marx's worldview, generally referred to as the materialist conception of history, also as historical materialism. I note that the materialist conception is often considered as the joint product of Marx and his friend and collaborator Frederick Engels; in this respect they are considered as a single personality. My focus is exclusively on Marx, the development of his worldview as one finds in his writings under his own name or in those written in collaboration with Engels. Marx himself never published an integrated and systematic account of the materialist conception. There is a page and half of summary statement in the preface to his 1859 *A Contribution to the Critique of Political Economy* and a brief account in the polemical work *The Poverty of Philosophy*. Engels wrote and published extensively on the subject.[1]

Marx's worldview was fully formulated before he was 30 years old.[2] The focus of this study is on the evolution of his thought up to that point, say, the writing (with Engels) of *The Communist Manifesto* (1848), though his later writings are referred to for clarification and elaboration.

Marx wrote extensively over a long period and on a very wide variety of topics, and he expressed his views with different degrees of emphasis, and at different levels of abstraction as the occasion demanded. This has made possible for different writers to place different, often conflicting, interpretations of his worldview. I have not tried to evaluate these interpretations. To do that would have meant writing a different kind of book. However, I have discussed in detail the issue that is central to many interpretations, the issue of the 'primacy' of the 'forces of production', or of the 'relations of production' or of the realm of thought, the 'superstructure'.

The development of Marx's political philosophy can be said to have started while he was a student at Berlin University. At the age of 19, he wrote to his father that Hegel's philosophy provided a powerful tool for changing the world.[3]

He took from Hegel two ideas that would be critical elements in the development of his thought.

First, in Hegel's system of thought society is conceptualised in organic terms, rejecting the idea that society is a voluntary civic association formed by autonomous, rational individuals to further their private ends. In opposition to this individualist standpoint, in Hegel's thought society and its institutions are seen as having evolved organically, individuals are seen to be related to each other as parts of an organism, and individual rationality and morality are considered as products of society.

Second, in the Hegelian view, history is a process of development, of organic growth, development taking place from lower to higher formations through a dialectical process. It is a rational process; there is an inherent logic that drives society forward without the aid of any extraneous factor.

The formation of Marx's own philosophical standpoint would develop with a critique of two other aspects of Hegel's thought. The first was Hegel's philosophical idealism. According to this viewpoint, reality as we know it has no independent existence, it is an external appearance of Idea, of thought.

Hegel considered that his idea of the ideal state (an ethical entity, morally superior to civil society, the sphere of private interest) had already been realised in countries of Western Europe (countries with developed capitalism). He saw his own philosophy as an idealised retrospective evaluation of the historical process that had brought about this ideal state and society.

Marx's first, and momentous, breakthrough in the development of his worldview came in his comprehensive critique of Hegel's political philosophy *Contribution to the Critique of Hegel's Philosophy of Law* [Right] (the *Hegel Critique*), written in 1843.[4] Here Marx followed the lead given in the recently published *Preliminary Theses on the Reform of Philosophy* by Feuerbach.[5]

In the *Theses*, Feuerbach reversed the Hegelian relationship between thought (consciousness, spirit, God) and reality, a relationship in which, as already noted, reality was merely a manifestation of thought. Feuerbach asserted the opposite: man was not an expression or attribute of God or spirit; on the contrary, God was a creation of human imagination. God was man's relinquished self. (This is the definition of man's alienation in the realm of religion.) This was the methodological insight Marx used to develop his own critique of Hegel's theory of the state and, indeed, his own worldview.

In the *Hegel Critique* Marx extended Feuerbach's concept of alienation (confined to the realm of religion) to politics. Marx argued that man is alienated in the realm of politics – the state is man's relinquished self. A year later he would extend this concept to the realm of economics: capital, a product of labour, is man's relinquished self. (See Chapter 4.) Man will really be free when he has overcome his self-alienation in all the three realms of life and reclaimed the powers that he has conferred on the institutions of his own creation.

In the spring and summer of 1844, Marx (he was now in Paris) undertook a serious study of the works of a large number of political economists. During this period, Marx made extensive notes on the works he read. A part of these notes was published for the first time in 1932. The editors of his collected works gave these notes the title of *The Economic and Philosophical Manuscripts of 1844*.

In *The Manuscripts*, Marx referred to, and quoted from, the works of numerous political economists, but I argue (Chapter 4) that the work that had the most significant and lasting impact on Marx's thought was *The Wealth of Nations* by Adam Smith. I suggest that the contribution from Adam Smith was of the same magnitude in the development of Marx's worldview as the inversion of Hegel he received from Feuerbach, the insight that made him a materialist.

Up till now Marx had been entirely ploughing the philosophical field. His conversion to materialism had resulted from the inversion of Hegel; he had only vaguely talked of private property and had equally vaguely referred to money as an 'alien being'; and, most interestingly, had attributed to the proletariat a leading role in changing the world because of its 'suffering' and because it was a 'universal class'. Now Marx moved into a different territory.

In *The Manuscripts*, for the first time Marx is dealing with capitalism, a distinct mode of production, with a class society where (as Smith had put it) the interests of the masters and their workers are not the same; the central social relation is that between capital and labour, and the leading role of the proletariat is now rooted in production. In *The Manuscripts* there is a great deal of discussion of alienation, but this is now related to the worker in production.

Further, in *The Manuscripts*, Marx took his first step in the formation of his own version of materialism, rejecting all earlier versions, including Feuerbach's. In the months that followed, the insights achieved in *The Manuscripts* were fully developed and articulated in his *Theses on Feuerbach*. This was in the spring of 1845. (Marx was now in Brussels, having been expelled from France.) This was the final breakthrough. Marx now had all the elements of his mature worldview.

The old versions of materialism lacked any dynamic element and therefore could not provide a basis for understanding historical development. Old materialism treated reality as given datum, objective, something 'out there'; according to it human knowledge, ideas, etc., are determined by human brains receiving some kind of mechanical impulses from outside. Mind, humanity, is treated as passive.

The new view does away with this dualism of reality and consciousness. Reality is created by human beings.

I have suggested that the first intimation of this revolutionary thought – a thought that forms the core of the new worldview – is contained in the remark that Adam Smith was the '[Martin] Luther of political economy'. Smith deserved this title because he had declared that the wealth of a nation was the product of its labour; because he had done away with 'this external, mindless objectivity of wealth' and discovered the 'subjective essence' of wealth. Wealth was no longer seen as a stock of precious metals, nor of endowments of existing goods, nor of natural resources. Smith had seen wealth as a flow of commodities produced by labour, year after year, and the productivity of labour as the cause of increase in the wealth of nations. Thus, wealth was not something 'out there', a given datum; it was labour embodied, labour materialised. Reality, in this case annual national product, is the creation of humankind.

This idea is extended to all reality when Marx makes the distinction between 'historical nature' and 'original nature', nature shaped by man and nature that man found when he first appeared on the scene. It is man, active man, the producer, who is the dynamic factor in historical development.

I have explained how this idea becomes the basis of Marx's general approach to the understanding of historical development. The starting point of the new conception is man's natural and social needs, and man trying to satisfy these needs through productive activity. Man's power of reasoning and his understanding of nature arise and develop out of this activity. Elements of the so-called superstructure – thought, politics, ideology, etc., arise as necessary adjustments that people make to the changing needs of production; they arise as responses to specific needs and problems.

Thus, every generation receives from the preceding generation a set of needs, and the means and instruments for satisfying these needs and elements of the superstructure. In satisfying these needs, new needs are created and also new instruments for satisfying them, as well as modifications, etc., of the elements of the inherited superstructure, modifications that are necessary adjustment for the production process. Epochal changes or changes in modes of production, take place when society is unable to make the institutional and social adjustments necessary for the progress of development. This conception is then used to explain the transition from feudalism to capitalism, and, further, to the projected movement from capitalism to socialism.

This (according to Marx) is a spontaneous process. The question now arises, can the conscious human agency (politics, the party, etc.) successfully intervene in this process so that the course of historical development will be different from what it would have been in the absence of such intervention? That is, can we consciously change the world? The short answer is that the conscious human agency (politics) can, and does, affect the course of events, but it can do so only within the limits of the inheritance received from the preceding generations. It is this inheritance that creates a certain potential. To change the world the conscious human agency must understand the nature of this potential and understand the limits within which it can act successfully. In reality, it may realise this potential or fail to do that. Things are not pre-determined (by technology or economic forces, etc.). And the future development depends on capabilities of the human agency – the capabilities that are conditioned but not pre-determined by the preceding development. (See Chapter 6, section 'The role of the conscious human agency in the process of development').

It will be noted that I have rejected the conventional interpretation of Marx's conception in which a clear separation is made between the 'base', made up of the 'forces of production', and the superstructure of thought, and in which the base is treated as an independent variable which determines the character of the dependent variable, the superstructure. (It is this relationship that supposedly makes the conception 'materialist'.) A popular textbook on political theory puts this interpretation in the following words:

> ... the forces of production – the methods of producing goods
> and distributing the products of industry – are always primary
> as compared with their secondary, ideological consequences.
> The material or economic forces are 'real' or substantial, while
> ideological relations are only apparent or phenomenal.[6]

Another author puts the conventional interpretation in the following words:

> On the side of materialism ... classical scientific materialism is
> reductive and determinist, and conceives of 'matter' as an inert
> substance subject to 'iron laws' of nature. For a Marxism under
> the influence of this tendency, the political and theoretical
> superstructure are epiphenomena of society's material base.
> Only that material base, the economy, and perhaps its most
> material aspect, technology has real causal agency.[7]

This interpretation then leads to the criticism that in practice it is impossible to distinguish between elements of the superstructure and those of the base and therefore Marx's conception cannot adequately explain historical development; that is, one cannot always tell whether an event was influenced or caused by forces of production or some element of the superstructure. To quote the textbook mentioned earlier again:

> In a tangle of social institutions it is meaningless to insist that
> some single change is always the 'cause' of all other changes.
> The truth is that Marx's distinction of superstructure and foun-

dation was not empirical. His model was Hegel's metaphysical distinction between appearance and reality, as is evident from his singular conclusion that every social problem must be soluble. (p.700)

Fundamentally, this interpretation is based on the assumed antithesis between 'things and consciousness' which, as we have seen, Marx rejected. Forces of production cannot be understood independently of men's knowledge, thought, ingenuity, etc. A locomotive by itself is not a force of production. The 'materialist' aspect of Marx's conception consists (as discussed in Chapter 6) in the claim that ideas have no history independently of men engaged in productive activity, and that man, consciousness, cannot create anything out of nothing.[8]

I have argued that the materialist conception does not offer a description of reality, nor is it a scientific law. It is a conceptual framework for understanding reality, the historical process. In the Afterword to the second edition of *Capital*, Marx referred to it as 'the materialist basis of my method' and in the preface to *A Contribution to the Critique of Political Economy* as 'the general result ... which ... served as a guiding thread for my studies'. He specifically denied that his worldview was a 'general historical-philosophical theory'. By implication, in this conception, there is no room for the view ('evolutionism') that all societies are inevitably moving towards a final destination, a communist society. Such a view would be un-empirical, suprahistorical, and therefore contrary to Marx's thought.

Marx did talk about 'stages' of development as different modes of production or social orders. But the only transition between modes of production discussed by him was from feudalism to capitalism, a discussion that was based on historical facts; and his discussion of the projected transition from capitalism to communism was based entirely on observed tendencies in the working of capitalism. He may have been wrong in giving greater weight to some observed tendencies than to others, but that of course is another matter. (These issues are discussed in detail in Chapter 6.)

I have suggested that there are certain important aspects of Marx's worldview that are ideologically neutral in the sense that they can be accepted and used by those who do not subscribe to his communist vision. In fact, many of his ideas have become part of the general social and economic thought.

On this point I can do no better than to quote a passage from Isaiah Berlin's *Karl Marx – His Life and Environment*:

> The scientific study of economic relations and their bearing on other aspects of the lives of communities and individuals began with the application of Marxist canons of interpretation. Previous thinkers – for example, Vico, Hegel, Saint-Simon –

drew up general schemata, but their direct results, as embodied in the gigantic systems of Comte or Spencer, are at once too abstract and vague, and as forgotten in our day as they deserve to be. The true father of modern economic history, and, indeed, of modern sociology, in so far as any one man may claim that title, is Karl Marx. If to have turned into truisms what had previously been paradoxes is a mark of genius, Marx was richly endowed with it. His achievements in this sphere are necessarily forgotten in proportion as their effects have become part of the permanent background of civilized thought.[9]

I may also add here what Joseph Schumpeter wrote:

Things economic and social move by their own momentum and the ensuing situations compel individuals and groups to behave in certain ways whatever they may wish to do – not indeed by destroying their freedom of choice but by shaping the choosing mentalities and by narrowing the list of possibilities from which to choose. If this is the quintessence of Marxism then we all of us have got to be Marxists.[10]

NOTES

1 For instance, his *Dialectics of Nature* and *Anti-Dühring*.
2 According to Joseph Schumpeter, 'at the age of 29, he [Marx] was in possession of all the essentials that make up the Marxist social science, the only important lacunae being in the field of technical economics.' *History of Economic Analysis*, George Allen & Unwin, London, 1954, p.388. And according to the editors' preface to volume 6 of the *Karl Marx Frederick Engels Collected Works* [MECW], Lawrence & Wishart, London, 1975, p.xxviii: 'With *The [Communist] Manifesto* the process of Marxism was... basically complete'. The same point is made by the German historian Golo Mann who writes: [In 1848] the political philosophy and revolutionary strategy named after him [Marx] was already complete in his mind.' *The History of Germany since 1789*, Penguin, Harmondsworth, 1974, p.143.
3 Georg Wilhelm Friedrich Hegel (1770-1831), German classical philosopher.
4 *Contribution to the Critique of Hegel's Philosophy of Law [Right]*, MECW, vol.3. Hegel's *Philosophie des Rechts* is translated by some writers as *Philosophy of Law* and others as *Philosophy of Right,*
5 Ludwig Andreas von Feuerbach (1804-1872), German materialist philosopher.
6 George Sabine and Thomas L. Thorson, *A History of Political Theory*, 4th edition, Holt, Rinehart and Winston, Fort Worth, 1973, p.699.
7 Roy Edgley, 'Dialectical Materialism' in John Eatwell, Murray Milgate and Peter Newman, eds., *The New Palgrave Marxian Economics*, Macmillan, London and Basingstoke, 1990, p.119.
8 This point is widely misunderstood. For instance, one author writes that the problem for Marxists is 'how to maintain the awareness of the active role of politics and ideas without abandoning their claim for the primacy of society's mode of production, claims which, after all, give Marxism its distinctiveness as a theory of the social world and of history.' S. H. Rigby, *Marxism and History – A Critical Introduction*, Manchester University Press, Manchester and New York, 1998, p.x.
9 A Galaxy Book, Oxford University Press, New York, 1959, p.144.
10 *Capitalism, Socialism & Democracy*, Routledge, London and New York, 1994, pp.129-30.

1

A Young Hegelian

Early formative years

Karl Marx was born on 5 May 1818 in Trier, a small, historical town in the Rhineland region of Germany. During the Napoleonic wars, the region was annexed by France and governed under the Napoleonic code. During this period, the region had full exposure to the principles of the French Enlightenment and Revolution. After the defeat of Napoleon, the region was incorporated into Prussia, governed under a monarchical, semi-feudal autocratic constitution. Though the Napoleonic reforms were abrogated they had left their mark on the intellectual climate of the region.

Marx's family, both from his father's and mother's side, came from a long line of Rabbis. His paternal grandfather was a Rabbi in Trier and, after his death, was succeeded in this position by his paternal uncle. His mother's family had a succession of Rabbis. Karl's father, Heinrich Marx, a prosperous lawyer in the town, had recently renounced his Jewish faith and converted to Protestantism.

One of eight children, Karl was deeply attached to his father, who took particular interest in his intellectual development. According to Marx's daughter Eleanor, Heinrich was a real Frenchman of the 18th century Enlightenment who knew his Voltaire and Rousseau by heart. Heinrich was also familiar with the ideas of the French socialist Saint-Simon. He was member of a literary society in Trier which also had as its member a Saint-Simonian who had published a pamphlet with the title *The Privileged Classes and the Working Classes*.

A more important influence than his father on young Karl was a neighbour, Baron Ludwig von Westphalen, a high Prussian official with aristocratic connections. A highly cultured man, the Baron took the young Marx – still a school boy – for long walks, discussing (according to Eleanor) Homer and Goethe with him. Later, at the age of 19, Karl would ask von Westphalen for the hand of his daughter Jenny in marriage, and receive consent. Marx would also dedicate his doctoral dissertation to the Baron, 'my fatherly friend', who had shown him that 'idealism is no illusion, but the true reality.' Von Westphalen's long discussions with the young pupil must have strengthened the young Marx's self-belief, a quality that remained with him all his life.

Karl went to the local school, the Royal Friedrich Wilhelm Gymnasium. The headmaster of the school was a man of liberal views and member of the local literary society. It is therefore possible that the general milieu of the school was dominated by Enlightenment liberalism.

Marx's school-leaving certificate noted his ability to interpret difficult passages in the classics, 'and in particular such passages where the difficulty lay less in the peculiarities of the language than in the subject matter and the relation of ideas'. It added that 'his Latin themes show richness of thought and a deep acquaintance with their subject, but are often over weighted with unsuitable matter.'[1]

Here two things are worth noting. In his school-leaving essay, titled 'The reflections of a young man on the choice of profession', we note the ambitions of the 17-year-old Marx 'to serve humanity'. He wrote: 'But the chief guide which must direct us in the choice of a profession is the welfare of mankind and our own perfection. It should not be thought that these two could be in conflict, that one would have to destroy the other; on the contrary, man's nature is so constituted that he can attain his own perfection only by working for the perfection, for the good of his fellow men.'[2] The entire essay is written in this high-minded tone.

Second, Marx refused to pay a farewell visit to the reactionary co-headmaster who had been appointed by the government to keep an eye on the liberal-minded headmaster. It was customary that after matriculating and before departing, students show their respect to senior staff by paying them a farewell visit. For this neglect, Marx was reprimanded by his father who had to make excuses on his behalf.

In the autumn of 1835, Marx was sent by his father to Bonn University to study law. Heinrich was keen that Karl should become a lawyer and, like himself, lead a respectable bourgeois life. Marx spent a year in Bonn attending lectures on jurisprudence, history of Roman law, Homer, Roman and Greek mythology and modern art.

Although Karl's university progress report described him as a 'diligent and attentive' student his father was unhappy with his progress with legal studies. Heinrich therefore arranged for him to be transferred to Berlin University, which the philosopher Ludwig Feuerbach had described as a 'workhouse' as compared to other German universities. In October 1836, Marx entered Berlin University where Hegel had been professor of philosophy until his death in 1831. Marx remained there until the end of March, 1841.

An Emotional Conversion

After a year at Berlin, Marx reported to his father on the progress of his studies. This he did in a letter, written during the night of 10/11 November 1837. This is an extraordinary letter. It gives us a remarkable insight into Marx's method of work, the range of his interests, his insatiable appetite for knowledge, capacity for hard work, and his remarkable ability to master difficult and complex ideas rapidly. I will quote from the letter at some length.[3]

Here the 19-year-old son opens his heart to his loving father and reports his conversion to Hegel's philosophy which he claims provides the key to understanding reality. The letter opens with the declaration:

> There are moments in one's life which are like frontier posts marking the completion of a period but at the same time clearly indicating direction... At such moments, however, a person becomes lyrical, for every metamorphosis is partly a swan song, partly the overture to a great new poem...

He tells his father that he had 'tried to elaborate philosophy of law covering the whole field of law.' The work ran to more than 300 pages. He goes into detail about what he had tried to achieve and what he had failed to achieve. 'Here the same opposition between what is and what ought to be stood out as a serious defect.' Then he tried his hand at a 'new system of metaphysical principles', but here 'I was once more compelled to recognise that it was wrong, like my previous efforts.'

There is much more in this vein. He reports on the enormous amount of reading he had done, both of the classics and of modern works, during the one year he had been at Berlin University. At the same time, he had translated Tacitus' *Germania* and Ovid's *Tristia*. And there is much more. He was also learning English and Italian by himself.

Then he turns to his study of Hegel's philosophy. At the beginning Hegel's 'grotesque craggy melody' did not appeal to him. However, later he returned to the master, and after 'fruitless labour' (during which he translated part of Aristotle's *Rhetoric*), he got to know him 'from beginning to end together with most of his disciples.' Now, 'all rich chords were silenced and I was seized with a veritable fury of irony as could easily happen after so much had been negated.' He had now 'arrived at the point of seeking the idea in reality itself. If previously the gods had dwelt above the earth, now they became its centre.' He had fathomed Hegel's dialectical method: 'The object itself must be studied in its development; arbitrary divisions must not be introduced, the rational character of the object itself must develop as something imbued with contradictions in itself and find its unity in itself.'

The metamorphosis had come like a great spiritual conversion, a conversion that had delivered him into 'the arms of the enemy'. In this febrile atmosphere 'my vexation made me quite incapable of thinking; I ran about madly in the garden' and 'rushed off to embrace every street-corner loafer.' Such was the intensity of the experience.

Heinrich Marx, who hated Hegel's philosophy, was not impressed by his son's 'musty excursions into all departments of knowledge' and 'senseless and inexpedient erudition'.[4] He died the following year (1838) fearful for his son's future.

We will see as we proceed that Hegel would be an immensely important influence on the development of Marx's world outlook. In fact, Marx's own political-philosophical standpoint will develop as an internal critique of Hegel's political philosophy; and Hegel's concept of the state will provide the basis of his vision of the future communist society. In his 1892 introduction to *Socialism: Utopian and Scientific*, Engels recalled his and Marx's intellectual debt to Hegel by saying that Hegel's conception of history provided the direct theoretical premise for the materialist outlook he and Marx later adopted.[5] Years later, Marx himself, in the Afterword to the second edition of *Capital*, said that he had extracted the 'rational core' of the 'great thinker's' concept of dialectics, which the latter had mystified, and that he had put Hegel, who was standing on his head, the right side up.

The Doctors' Club and the Doctoral Dissertation

In the letter mentioned above, Marx also informed his father that he had joined a Doctors' Club, a discussion group of writers and university lecturers who were members of the Young Hegelian movement. The movement was led by Bruno Bauer, a theology lecturer at Berlin University. Other prominent members included Karl Köppen, a history teacher, Georg Jung, a lawyer, and Arnold Ruge, a radical philosopher. Marx, who had hardly been one year at Berlin University, and not yet 20, soon moved to the centre of the movement, becoming friends with its leading figures, including Bauer and Köppen. Köppen, ten years older than Marx, would later (1840) dedicate his book on the life of Frederick the Great of Prussia to 'my friend Karl Marx of Trier'.

The Young Hegelian movement can be said to have been initiated with the publication, in 1835, of David Strauss' *Life of Jesus Critically Examined*. Strauss argued that the Bible should be subjected to normal intellectual inquiry. He claimed that Christianity was one stage in human progress, like Judaism and other religions before it. These ideas presented a direct intellectual challenge to the prevailing conservative interpretations of Hegel's philosophy of history that claimed that Protestant Christianity represented the culmination of the development of the state and of human society.

Against this view, the Young Hegelians emphasised the Hegelian idea that institutions that served useful purposes and were thus historically justified at one stage could become obsolete and irrelevant through their own development.

Further, they argued that it was obvious that the semi-feudal, autocratic Prussian state— officially a Protestant Christian state – was not the end of history; that the dialectic of development had some way to go yet. The Young Hegelians favoured a liberal, constitutional monarchy. This objective was to be pursued through philosophical criticism, through advancing self-consciousness. At the time of Marx's student days in Berlin, these discussions provided the context of his intellectual development.

It appears that Marx started his serious studies for his doctoral thesis sometime in 1839. His reading notes and preparatory material for the thesis are compiled in seven notebooks he made at the time. The method he adopted in the writing of these notes (a method he will follow in his later works) took the form of copying excerpts from the books he read, writing a critical commentary on these excerpts, and then putting down his own ideas developed on the subject based on his commentaries.

The choice of the subject for the thesis – *Difference between the Democritean and Epicurean Philosophy of Nature* – seems to have been guided by a number of different considerations. It is obvious from his letter to his father quoted earlier that Marx had little interest in the study of law and becoming a lawyer. His interest lay in philosophy. His friends, Bauer and Köppen in particular, had strong interest in ancient Greek philosophy and it is likely that they had some influence on the choice of the subject. The choice was also appropriate for the pursuit of an academic career. (Bauer had suggested to him it would be foolish if he were to devote himself to a practical career.) Bauer was hoping to get a chair in philosophy at the university of Bonn and was keen that his young friend should join him there as a colleague. It is equally likely that Marx chose this subject because he was keen to strengthen his grounding in philosophy by a serious study of the philosophical legacy of ancient Greece.

Later commentators have been surprised that Marx should have considered Epicurus (341-270 B.C.) a greater thinker than Democritus (c. 460- c. 370 BC) who is widely regarded as the more profound thinker. From Marx's discussion it is evident that what attracted him to Epicurus was the latter's 'energising principle' – the activist element – in his philosophy which Democritus' materialism lacked. It is this principle that enabled Epicurus to defy religion. In the foreword to the dissertation, Marx wrote:

> Philosophy, as long as a drop of blood shall pulse in its world-subduing and absolutely free heart, will never grow tired of answering its adversaries with the cry of Epicurus: 'Not the man who denies the gods worshipped by the multitude, but

he who affirms of the gods what the multitude believes about them, is truly impious.'[6]

In the dissertation Marx contrasts the views of the two philosophers on the subject of 'necessity'. According to Democritus necessity is 'fate and law, providence and the creator of the world'. For Epicurus (Marx quotes):

> Necessity, as introduced by some as the absolute ruler, *does not exist*... It would be better to follow the myth about the gods than to be a slave to the *heimarmene* [destiny] of the physicists... It is a misfortune to live in necessity, but to live in necessity is not a necessity. On all sides many short and easy paths to freedom are open.[7]

Marx's admiration for Epicurus remained undiminished over time – in *The German Ideology* (1845-46), written with Engels, he referred to him as the genuine radically-enlightened mind of antiquity.[8]

In the foreword to the dissertation, Marx quotes from Aeschylus' *Prometheus Bound*. where Prometheus ('the most eminent saint and martyr in the philosophical calendar') tells Hermes, the servant of the gods:

> Be sure of this, I would not change my state
> Of evil fortune for your servitude.
> Better to be the servant of this rock
> Than to be faithful boy to Father Zeus.[9]

One wonders if the 23-year-old Marx is beginning to think of himself as a latter-day Prometheus.

Early in April 1841, Marx submitted his dissertation to the University of Jena. He had been advised not to submit it at Berlin University where, with the arrival of a new professor, the philosopher F. W. von Schelling, atmosphere at the university had become extremely hostile to Young Hegelians, in fact to all Hegelians. Marx received his doctorate in philosophy from the University of Jena on 15 April, in less than two weeks of the submission of the thesis.

Marx had intended to enlarge his dissertation for publication, but for reasons that are not clear, the plan did not materialise. Late in 1841 and early 1842 Marx wrote the draft of a new preface to the dissertation, which presumably he now planned to publish in its original form. This attempt also bore no fruit.

As indicated, Marx had hoped, with the encouragement of Bruno Bauer, to pursue an academic career. Bauer, who was teaching theology at the university of Berlin was, in 1839, moved to a teaching position in Bonn University. There was an understanding between him and the Minister of Culture, the reform-minded Karl Siegmund Altenstein, that after a few months he would be given a permanent professorship at Bonn. Bauer, had thought that once he was installed in the professorial chair he would secure an appointment for Marx. However, with the death in May 1840 of Altenstein, and the appointment of a new minister of culture who was particularly hostile to Young Hegelians, and perhaps also because of Bauer's continuing attacks on the Gospels, any chance of Bauer obtaining a professorship, and with it any possibility of Marx getting an academic appointment, were extinguished. Bauer was suspended from his post in March 1842. Marx now had to look for another career.

Interest in Politics

Arnold Ruge, the Young Hegelian whom Marx had known in Berlin (and who had also failed to obtain an academic position), had founded a radical journal, the *Hallische Jahrbücher* in 1838. It published contributions from David Strauss, Bauer and other Young Hegelians. In the summer of 1841, Ruge was ordered by the government in Berlin to submit the journal, which was published in Leipzig, to Prussian censorship. The penalty for refusal would be the prohibition of the journal in the territories controlled by Prussia. In response to this threat, Ruge moved the publication of the journal, now renamed *Deutsche Jahrbücher*, to Dresden (out of Prussian jurisdiction). The new journal, whose first issue appeared on the 1 July 1841, adopted a politically sharper tone than its predecessor. Marx told Ruge that he would put all his energies into supporting his new journal.

Towards the end of December 1841 (after having spent six months with Bauer in Bonn), Marx went to Trier to be with von Westphalen who was seriously ill. He stayed there with the Westphalen family until von Westphalen's death in March (1842). During this period, Marx continued his studies and also started to take interest in politics. He wrote an article on the order which the new King (Frederick William VI who succeeded to the throne in 1840) had issued apparently aimed at relaxing the existing censorship restrictions. With a letter dated 10 February, Marx sent this article to Ruge for publication in the *Deutsche Jahrbücher*. This was a sharp attack on the royal order. Written in trenchant pamphleteering style, the article brought out the order's inconsistencies. This was Marx's first foray into political writing.

Within two weeks of receiving the article, Ruge informed Marx that because of difficulties with the censor the article could not be published. The article was later published in 1843 in *Anekdota Philosophica*, a symposium, published by Ruge in Switzerland. Other contributors to this volume included Ludwig Feuerbach, Karl Köppen and Ruge himself.

In the same letter, Marx suggested to Ruge that he would like to review two books for the *Deutsche Jahrbücher*. One of them had already been reviewed by Feuerbach, but Marx thought that it merited further examination. He also informed Ruge that he had 'come to the end of voluminous works', but he did not give any indication of the nature of these works.

A little over three weeks later, in a letter (5 March 1842) to Ruge, he refers to an article of his, 'Treatise on Christian Art', which should have appeared in a work jointly written by him and Bauer.[10] In this work they had intended to argue, on the basis of Hegel's aesthetics and philosophy, that the Young Hegelians, not Old Hegelians, were the true inheritors of the master's spirit. However, their cooperation on this project had come to end because while Bauer confined himself to a radical criticism of Christian theology, Marx was now increasingly becoming interested in linking philosophy with political questions. There was as yet no open breach between the two, but politically and intellectually, Marx was getting further away from his friend. Marx offered to send this article to Ruge for publication in the forthcoming *Anekdota Philosophica*.

In the same letter Marx informs Ruge that he is writing another article which he would submit for publication in *Deutsche Jahrbücher*. This article, Marx tells Ruge 'is a criticism of Hegelian philosophy of natural law, insofar as it concerns the *internal political system*' (Marx's emphasis). 'The central point', he writes, 'is the struggle against constitutional monarchy as a hybrid which from beginning to end contradicts and abolishes itself.' He says that he would send both these articles 'for your examination but before that they would require some corrections'. He adds:

> The fact is that my future father-in-law, Herr von Westphalen, lay on his death-bed for three months and died the day before yesterday. During this period, therefore, it was impossible to do anything properly.[11]

This letter is the first occasion that Marx, now 23 years old, refers to his proposed critique of Hegel's political philosophy. Though at this stage, Marx's general thinking is still in the Hegelian frame, we may conjecture that during his stay with the Westphalen family in Trier, he had started to re-examine his relationship with his old mentor. This paper was not delivered to Ruge for publication, but it seems reasonable to think that this draft, or what is more likely, the notes written for it, would form the basis of the 130-page *Contribution to the Critique of Hegel's Philosophy of Law* [*Right*] he would write in the summer of 1843. It is also likely that the notes for this paper were part of the 'voluminous works' referred to in the letter of 10 February.

Marx's correspondence with Ruge at this time clearly indicates his growing interest in politics. In a letter dated 20 March (1842), he refers to a Prussian government order, issued two days earlier, according to which judicial proceedings for certain purposes in Rhineland were to be held in secret. Marx writes:

> Prussia has declared with complete naivety that publicity of

court proceedings would jeopardise the prestige and credit of Prussian officials. This is an extremely frank admission.' He adds that he would like to prove that 'Prussia cannot introduce publicity and publicising, for free courts and unfree state are incompatible... Similarly, Prussia should be highly praised for its piety, for transcendental state and a positive religion go together, just as a pocket icon does with a Russian swindler.[12]

In the same letter, Marx offers his apologies for not having sent the articles he had promised in his letter of 5 March. The article on Christian art , he informs Ruge, must be redone. Since it was written for a book he had planned to write with Bauer it suffered from 'the irksome constraint of the Hegelian exposition.' He promises to send the article by mid-April if Ruge could wait so long. He also apologises (in the letter of 25 March) for not having sent the article criticising Hegel's philosophy of law as this too was conceived for the book that was to be written with Bauer, and thus needed further thought.

Marx is clearly conscious of the fact that while he keeps promising Ruge these articles, he is unable to deliver them. In a letter written from Bonn on 27 April (1842), he asks Ruge not to 'become impatient if my contributions are delayed for a few days more – but *only for a few* days... I have almost finished. I shall send you four articles: 1) 'On Religious Art', 2) 'On the Romantics', 3) 'The Philosophical Manifesto of the Historical School of Law', 4) 'The Positivist Philosophers'. The article on religious art had by now grown into a book, but he would summarise it for publication in *Deutsche Jahrbücher*. He also informs Ruge that he had sent a long article to the newly launched Cologne newspaper, the *Rheinische Zeitung*, in connection with the Rhineland assembly debates on press laws. In it he had 'returned to the question of censorship and freedom of the press, examining it from other viewpoints'.[13] This article (the first writing of Marx to appear in print) was published in the newspaper on 5 May 1842.

A Digression on Method

This will not be the last time that Marx will test the patience of a publisher. None of the promised articles was delivered to Ruge for publication. Of the promised articles mentioned above, only the one on the 'philosophical manifesto of the historical school of law' was published. It appeared in the *Rheinische Zeitung* of 9 August 1842. As mentioned earlier, his draft or notes on Hegel would (as I conjectured earlier) be developed during the summer of 1843 into a long critique on Hegel's philosophy of law. (This monograph was published for the first time in 1927). The other papers he was working on at this time are not extant. Marx was not a writer who was rushing to the press.

We have here a glimpse of Marx's method of work that will remain with him all his life. It is this approach to his work that was responsible for the inordinate delays in the publication of his magnum opus, *Capital*. The method consisted in seeing ideas in their inter-connectedness with other ideas, to see things in their *totality*. (Something he had taken from Hegel, as he informed his father in the letter referred to earlier.) Nine years before the publication of the first volume of *Capital*, in a letter dated 22 February, 1858, Marx wrote to the German Social Democratic leader Ferdinand Lassalle:

> I will tell you how things stand with my work in economics. I have in fact had the final draft to hand for several months. But the progress is very slow, because things on which one has concentrated one's study for many years always produces something new when you think you have finished it, and demands new consideration.[14]

In a letter of 31 July, 1865 (two years before the publication of the first volume of *Capital*), he made the same point to Engels:

> I cannot make up my mind to send anything off before I have the whole thing lying in front of me. Whatever shortcomings they may have, the advantage of my works is that they form an artistic whole, and I can only achieve that by my practice of never having them printed before I have them *complete* in front of me. The Jakob Grimm method is impossible for this and only works for books which are not formed dialectically.[15]

Lying in front of him, when he was finishing the first volume of *Capital*, were the drafts of the second and third volumes of *Capital* and three volumes of the *Theories of Surplus Value* and the manuscript that was later given the title *Grundrisse*. None of these works was published in his lifetime.

It is this method that gives Marx's thought the unity and coherence that is difficult to find in the work of any other social, political or economic thinker. This point is effectively made by Joseph Schumpeter, who wrote:

> The difficulty is that in Marx's case we lose something that is essential to understanding him when we cut up his system into component propositions and assign separate niches to each, as our mode of procedure requires. To some extent this is so with every author: the whole is always more than the sum of the parts. But it is only in Marx's case that the loss we suffer by neglecting this is of vital importance, because the totality of his vision, as a totality, asserts its right in every detail and is precisely the source of the intellectual fascination experienced by everyone, friend as well as foe, who makes a study of him.[16]

The *Rheinische Zeitung*

Let us return to the story where we left it. I referred earlier to Marx's increasing interest in political issues of the day; at the same time, he had also become interested in practical politics. While living in Bonn, he had joined a group of intellectuals (some of them Young Hegelians) and liberal-minded businessmen in Cologne, the capital of Rhineland-Westphalia. The leading intellectuals in the group or 'the Cologne Circle', as it was called , included Georg Jung, whom Marx had known from his Berlin days, and Moses Hess, a writer who had studied philosophy in Paris where he had adopted socialist ideas. Marx made a strong impression on this group. Jung described him as one who had 'one of the acutest minds' he had known, while Hess compared him with the great thinkers of the Enlightenment.[17]

Some members of this Circle, in particular Jung and Hess, persuaded some of the wealthy members of the group to finance the launch of a newspaper that would advocate progressive policies. Marx was invited to join the paper as a contributor. The first issue of the newspaper, the *Rheinische Zeitung*, appeared on 1 January 1842.

The *Rheinische Zeitung* was not intended by its shareholders to be a radical newspaper. Its general outlook could be described as bourgeois-liberal, its masthead carried the words 'For politics, commerce and industry'. It advocated revival of the reforms introduced by Napoleon during the French occupation, supported economic and political unification of Germany and called for polices to support industrialisation. In the first instance, the financial backers of the paper offered its editorship to Friedrich List, the famous German economist who advocated protectionist policies to support the nascent German industry. He declined on health grounds. Under the influence of Moses Hess, and with the support of Marx, a Young Hegelian friend of Marx, Adolf Rutenberg, was appointed to the job. Hess was appointed assistant editor.

As noted earlier, with his first contribution to this newspaper in May (1842), Marx had launched himself on a journalistic career. From now on he became increasingly involved in the editorial work of the newspaper. By August, he was practically editing the paper. In October he was appointed editor-in-chief. This was after Rutenberg was sacked under pressure from the Prussian government. The shareholders were, in fact, glad to get rid of Rutenberg as his competence as editor was increasingly coming into question.

A letter to Dagobert Oppenheim, the director in charge of policy, (dated 30 November 1842) shows the very practical and business-like manner in which Marx was running the paper. Referring to some of the strident contributions to the newspaper from firebrand Young Hegelians, Marx wrote:

> General and theoretical considerations on the constitution of the state are more suitable for learned reviews than for news-

papers. The true theory must be expanded and developed in relation to concrete facts and the existing state of affairs. Therefore striking an attitude against the present pillars of the state could only result in tightening of the censorship and even the suppression of the paper... In any case we are annoying a large number, perhaps even the majority, of liberals engaged in political activity who have assumed the thankless and painful task of conquering liberty step by step within limits imposed by the constitution, while we, comfortably ensconced in abstract theory, point out to them their contradictions... I consider it absolutely indispensable that the *Rheinische Zeitung* should not be directed by its contributors but on the contrary that it should direct *them*.[18]

The newspaper flourished under the leadership of Marx; its circulation doubled within the first five months of his becoming editor. Some years later, an observer recalled:

All the young, fresh, free-thinking or (as the friends of the government complained) revolutionary talent that Prussia and Germany possessed took refuge here. Fighting with a great variety of weapons, now earnest, now mocking, now learned, now popular, today in prose, tomorrow in verse, they formed a phalanx against which the censorship and police struggled in vain...[19]

On 21 January, 1843, the Prussian government decided to suppress the newspaper though the decision was not implemented until 1 April. The decision to close down the paper resulted in a sharp rise in its circulation. Numerous citizens of the Rhineland sent petitions to the king to reverse the decision to ban the paper. A deputation of Cologne businessmen travelled to Berlin to plead with the king, but was refused audience. It was widely believed that the immediate reason for the suppression of the paper was the publication of a series of articles on the condition of Mosel peasants and the brutal repression of their protests.

Marx, however, had already decided to resign. The *Rheinische Zeitung* of 18 March 1843 carried the following announcement:

The undersigned declares that, owing to the *present conditions of censorship*, he has retired as from today from the editorial board of the *Rheinische Zeitung*. Cologne, March 17 1843. Dr Marx.

Four days earlier he had written to Ruge: 'As far as the *Rheinische Zeitung* is concerned I would not remain *under any conditions*; it is impossible for me to write under Prussian censorship or to live in the Prussian atmosphere.'[20]

The day after Marx resigned, the censor reported to his superiors in Berlin:

> The *spiritus rector* of the whole undertaking, Dr. Marx, definitely retired yesterday, and Oppenheim, on the whole a real moderate though insignificant man, took over the editorship … I am very pleased at this and today I had to spend hardly a quarter of the usual time on the censorship.

He suggested that since Marx had departed, the *Rheinische Zeitung* might now be allowed to continue publication. The authorities in Berlin did not respond.[21]

Break with Young Hegelians

The period of Marx's editorship of the *Rheinische Zeitung* also saw the beginning of his break with his former Young Hegelian friends. A number of members of the Berlin Doctors' Club that Marx had joined as a student, had from early 1842, formed a circle called 'Die Freien' (The Free). They had adopted an ultra-radical, anarchist standpoint, demanding, for instance, the dissolution of the family, private property and the state. According to the biographer of Marx referred to earlier, moving away from philosophical discussion that the Doctors' Club was set up to promote, they organised 'ragging processions', 'created scandalous scenes in brothels and taverns', thus hopelessly compromising the cause they professed to uphold.[22]

As indicated earlier, as editor, Marx found it more and more difficult to accommodate their articles, which were increasingly becoming sloppier in style. In a short article published in the newspaper on 29 November (1842), Marx completed his breach with the Free. He wrote: 'The Free are compromising the cause and the party of freedom by their political romanticism… Rowdiness and blackguardism must be loudly and resolutely repudiated in a period which demands serious, manly and sober-minded persons for the achievement of its lofty aims.'[23]

The following day, he wrote to Ruge about his breach with the Free. He wrote:

> As you already know, every day the censorship mutilates us mercilessly, so that frequently the newspaper is hardly able to appear. Because of this, a mass of articles by the 'Free' have perished. But I have allowed myself to throw out as many articles as the censor, for Meyen [a leader of the Free] and Co. sent us heaps of scribblings, pregnant with revolutionising the

world and empty of ideas, written in slovenly style and sea-
soned with a little atheism and communism (which these gen-
tlemen have never studied).

He continued:

> I demanded of them less vague reasoning, magniloquent
> phrases and self-satisfied self-adoration, and more definite-
> ness, more attention to the actual state of affairs, more expert
> knowledge. I stated that I regard it as inappropriate, indeed
> even immoral, to smuggle communist and socialist doctrines,
> hence a new world outlook, into incidental theatrical criti-
> cisms, etc., and that I demand a quite different and more thor-
> ough discussion of communism, if it should be discussed at
> all. I requested further that religion should be criticised in the
> framework of criticism of political conditions rather than that
> political conditions should be criticised in the framework of
> religion...; for religion in itself is without content, *it owes its
> being not to heaven but to earth, and with the abolition of distorted
> reality, of which it is the theory, it will collapse of itself.*[24] (Emphasis
> added.)

We may note here the first intimation of his materialist approach that Marx
will adopt later.

First Brush with the Idea of Communism

It is also during this period that Marx had his first serious brush with the
idea of communism or socialism. Marx was of course well aware of the subject matter of communism. And, as noted earlier, there were articles from
'the Free' Hegelians propounding socialism and anarchism which Marx as
editor had to deal with. But now, as editor of the *Rheinische Zeitung*, he faced
a challenge to which he had to respond.

Just about the time Marx took over as editor, the *Rheinische Zeitung* published a report of the proceedings of a conference of scholars from France,
Britain, Germany and other European countries in Strasbourg. One of the
sections of the conference discussed a proposal from some followers of the
French socialist thinker Charles Fourier for improving the social conditions
of the poor. One of the speakers compared the proletariat's struggle against
private property at the time with the struggle of the bourgeoisie against feudalism at the time of the French Revolution of 1789. This caused the *Allgemeine Zeitung,* an Augsburg newspaper with wide circulation, to charge the
Rheinische Zeitung with having communist sympathies.

Having little knowledge of socialist ideas at this time, Marx was unable to take a stand one way or another and responded the only sensible way open to him. He wrote:

> The *Rheinische Zeitung*, which does not admit that communist ideas in their present form possess even *theoretical reality*, and therefore can still less desire their *practical realisation*, or even consider it possible, will subject these ideas to thoroughgoing criticism. But if the lady of Augsburg demanded more, and was capable of more than smooth-sounding phrases, it would be obvious to her that such writings as those of [French socialists] Leroux, Considerant, and above all the sharp-witted work by Proudhon, cannot be criticised on the basis of superficial flashes of thought, but only after long and profound study.

But Marx showed where his social sympathies lay:

> That the estate that today owns nothing *demands* to share in the wealth of the middle classes is a fact which, without the talk at Strasbourg, and in spite of Augsburg's silence, is obvious to everyone in Manchester, Paris and Lyons [industrial centres that had experienced working class agitation]. Does the lady of Augsburg believe that her displeasure and silence have refuted the facts of the time?[25]

Towards the *Hegel Critique*

During his association with the *Rheinische Zeitung*, Marx wrote a large number of articles for the newspaper, most of them from a developing theoretical perspective. According to a recent biographer of Marx, they 'can be best understood as exercises in applied philosophy.'[26] Many of these were not published because of censorship restrictions. Those that were published dealt with a variety of issues, such as the freedom of the press, conditions of poor peasants in the Moselle valley and laws against theft of deadwood in forests.

The theoretical perspective of these articles was provided by two ideas. First, Marx accepted the Hegelian idea of the state (or community), rejecting thereby the principle of individualism that underlies the social contract theory which sees society as a voluntary association, the result of individual choices. For instance, in one of the articles published in the *Rheinische Zeitung*, Marx defined the idea of the 'rational' state (community) as follows:

> Whereas the earlier philosophers of constitutional law proceeded in their account of the formation of the state from the instincts, either of ambition or gregariousness, or even from

reason, though not social reason, but reason of the individual, the more ideal and profound view of recent philosophy proceeds from the idea of the whole. It looks on the state as the great organism, in which legal, moral and political freedom must be realised, and in which the individual citizen in obeying the laws of the state obeys the natural laws of his own reason.[27]

In another article, Marx expressed the same idea, referring to the state as 'a moral and rational commonweal' (*Gemeinwesen*).[28] The reason – social reason – that guides the state is the same thing as the collective intelligence of the people (*Volksintelligenz*), the spirit of the people (*Volksgeist*).[29]

Second, though Marx was still thinking within the frame of Hegelian philosophy, there was developing in his mind increasing tension between this outlook and the reality he observed around him. This reality differed sharply from the Hegelian ideal. It consisted, among other things, of the feudal, autocratic Prussian state, domination of the landowning class over the legislative bodies, and the oppression experienced by peasants. There was clearly a discrepancy between reality and philosophy, between the actual state and the 'rational' state.

This new realisation is particularly obvious in his two articles, one on debates in the Assembly on the 'pilfering' of wood in forests by poor people, and in his defence of the *Rheinische Zeitung* correspondent who had reported on the condition of Mosel peasants. The law on wood pilfering abrogated a traditional right of 'the poor, politically and socially propertyless' people in the interest of the landowning class.[30]

The second article was written in response to a government order to the newspaper accusing it of distorting facts about conditions of Mosel peasants, and demanding answers to five specific questions. Marx met the challenge and planned to write a series of six articles on the subject, but the newspaper was banned soon after he had published the second. (It was widely believed that these articles were the proximate cause of the ban. The ban came one week after the publication of the second instalment.)

Writing 17 years later, in the preface to *A Contribution to the Critique of Political Economy*, Marx recalled that this was the first time he realised the significance of 'material interests' and that it was this realisation that led him to the pursuit of economic questions.

Marriage and Further Study

In his letter of 25 January 1843 to Ruge, Marx had already indicated that he had come to the conclusion that because of censorship restrictions it would be impossible for him to work in Germany. After much discussion it was decided that a monthly journal, *Deutsch-Französische Jahrbücher*, with a 'French heart and German head' (French politics and German philosophy), publishing contributions from progressive French and German intellectuals would be published in Paris. They would co-edit the journal. Ruge, who was a person of independent means and was making a substantial investment of his own in the enterprise, assured Marx that he would receive a salary at which he and his wife should be able to live in reasonable comfort.

Marx went to Kreuznach where he and his fiancée Jenny were married on 19 June (1843). After a month's honeymoon with his new wife, Marx settled down for intensive study. Here he resumed his work on his Hegel critique and articles for the proposed journal.

In October, Marx and his wife arrived in Paris. Their life-long exile had begun.

NOTES

1 *MECW*, 1:643.
2 Ibid. p.8.
3 Ibid. pp.10-21.
4 Ibid. p.688.
5 *Karl Marx and Frederick Engels Selected Works* Foreign Languages Publishing House, Moscow, 1958, vol. 2, p. 132. (*MESW*, 2:132.)
6 *MECW*, 1:30
7 Ibid. pp.42-43.
8 Marx wrote: Epicurus 'was the true Enlightener of antiquity; he openly attacked the ancient religion, and it was from him, too, that the atheism of the Romans, insofar as it existed, was derived. For this reason, too, Lucretius praised Epicurus as the hero who was the first to overthrow the gods and trample religion underfoot; for this reason among all church leaders, from Plutarch to Luther, Epicurus has always had the reputation of being the atheist philosopher par excellence, and was called a swine...' *MECW*, 5:141-42.
9 *MECW*, 1: 30-31.
10 *MECW*, 1:382.
11 Ibid. p.383.
12 Ibid. p.384.
13 Ibid. p.387.
14 *Letters on 'Capital' by Karl Marx & Frederick Engels* (translated by Andrew Drummond), New Park Publications, London, 1983, p.51.
15 Ibid. p.96.
16 Joseph A. Schumpeter, *History of Economic Analysis*, George Allan & Unwin, London, 1954, p.384.
17 Gareth Stedman Jones, *Karl Marx – Greatness and Illusion*, Allen Lane, UK, 2016, p. 106.
18 Quoted in David McLellan, *Karl Marx – His Life and Thought*, Paladin, St. Albans, Herts., 1977, p.52.
19 Ibid. p.53.
20 *MECW*, 1:400.
21 Quoted in F. Mehring, *Karl Marx – The Story of his Life*, George Allen & Unwin, London, 1966 , p.51.
22 Ibid. p.45.
23 *MECW*, 1:287.
24 Ibid. p.393-94.
25 Ibid. p.220.
26 Gareth Stedman Jones, p.108.
27 *MECW*, 1:.202
28 Ibid. p.363.
29 It is interesting that the expression *Gemeinwesen* was used by Engels, in a letter to Bebel in May 1875, to describe the future communist society.
30 *MECW*, 1:.230.

2

The Paris Months

Deutsch-Französische Jahrbücher

When Marx arrived in Paris he brought with him from Kreuznach the monograph containing his critique of Hegel (the *Hegel Critique*), and an article with the title 'On the Jewish Question'. On arrival in Paris he wrote another article, 'Contribution to the Critique of Hegel's Philosophy of Law: Introduction'. Both these articles appeared in the first (and the only) issue of the *Deutsch-Französische Jahrbücher* in February (1844). The *Hegel Critique* was not published during Marx's life, though writing some 15 years later, in the preface to *A Contribution to the Critique of Political Economy* (1859), he referred to it as representing an important stage in the evolution of his materialist outlook.

Although Marx had taken this first crucial step in the formation of his materialist outlook, he had as yet no clear idea of the kind of society – 'the new world' – he was striving for. In a letter to Arnold Ruge, he spoke of the 'human world of democracy' but it is not clear what he meant by this expression. In September, one month before his arrival in Paris (by which time he had completed his *Hegel Critique*), he wrote to Ruge:

> For although no doubt exists on the question of 'whence', all the greater confusion prevails on the question of 'whither'.

Marx wished to find 'the new world' through criticism of the old one.

> But, if constructing the future and settling everything for all times are not our affair, it is all the more clear what we have to

accomplish at present. I am referring to ruthless criticism of all that exists, ruthless both in not being afraid of the results it arrives at and in the sense of being just as little afraid of conflict with the powers that be.[1]

On communism, he had an open mind. In the same letter to Ruge, he wrote:

> Thus, communism, in particular, is a dogmatic abstraction; in which connection, however, I am not thinking of some imaginary and possible communism, but actually existing communism as taught by Cabet, Dezamy, Weitling, etc. This communism is itself only a special expression of the humanistic principle, an expression which is still infected by its antithesis – the private system [individualism]. Hence the abolition of private property and communism are by no means identical, and it is not accidental but inevitable that communism has seen other socialist doctrines – such as those of Fourier, Proudhon, etc. – arising to confront it because it is itself only a special, one-sided realisation of the socialist principle.

He did not wish to approach the problems facing Germany by confronting them with some ready-made system such as the one presented in the French socialist Etienne Cabet's utopian communist tract *Journey to Icaria*.[2]

We will see in the next chapter that despite what Marx is saying here, around this time when he completed his article 'On the Jewish Question', he had already taken a decisive step towards the idea of socialism or communism. The conversion to the idea of communism will take place during the Paris months; by the end of the period he would have worked out the outlines of his materialist and communist outlook.

When Marx arrived in Paris, Ruge was already there making arrangements for the publication of the *Deutsch-Französische Jahrbücher*. Both Marx and Ruge approached the launch of the journal with great anticipation. Ruge declared:

> It is in Paris that we shall live our victories and defeats. Even our philosophy, the field where we are in advance of our time, will only be able to triumph when proclaimed in Paris and impregnated with the French spirit.[3]

And Marx wrote to Ruge:

> ... then give me your hand, so that we may begin again from the beginning. Let the dead bury their dead and mourn them. On the other hand, it is enviable to be the first to enter the new

life alive; that is to be our lot.[4]

As co-editor of the journal, Marx attempted to enlist the support of Feuer-bach, the pre-eminent radical philosopher in Germany at the time, asking him to contribute to the new journal. In his letter, Marx noted that he had inferred from his earlier writings that he had something interesting to say about the philosopher Schelling – this 'windbag' who had not only 'been able to unite philosophy and theology, but philosophy and diplomacy too.' Feuerbach was just the man for the job as he was 'Schelling in reverse'. And he concluded with a touch of flattery (that was completely out of character): 'Although she does not know you, my wife sends greetings. You would not believe how many followers you have among the fair sex.'[5]

Feuerbach, who was living the life of a recluse in the country, agreed with Marx's assessment of the political implications of Schelling's philoso-phy, but declined his invitation. He took the view that time was not yet ripe for transition from theory to practice.

The journal had been conceived as (as Marx had put it) an organ of the 'Franco-German alliance'. Invitations had been sent to prominent figures on the French Left, such as Pierre-Joseph Proudhon, Pierre Leroux, Etienne Cabet and Louis Blanc. But none of them responded positively. The first and the only issue, that appeared towards the end of February (1844), was thus an entirely German affair, and it made no impact at all on the French politi-cal scene. The French thinkers on the Left, it seemed, were not yet ready for a Franco-German alliance.

On the German side, contributors to the journal included Marx, the po-ets Heinrich Heine and Georg Herwegh, F. C. Bernays, a radical journal-ist, Moses Hess and Frederick Engels. The two articles of Marx published in the journal have already been mentioned – 'On the Jewish Question', a commentary on his old friend Bruno Bauer's article of the same title, and 'Introduction' to the *Hegel Critique*. Engels contributed two articles, 'Outline of Contribution to a Critique of Political Economy' and 'The Condition of England: Past and Present by Thomas Carlyle'. The first article greatly ap-pealed to Marx – he included a short summary of this paper in his *Paris Notebooks* – and it can be said to have laid the basis of their future collabora-tion and friendship.

In Berlin, the authorities viewed the journal as a seditious enterprise. (Marx's letters to Ruge, concerning the journal and published in it, could alone have justified this view.) The import of the journal's copies into Prus-sia was banned, and nearly two-thirds of the 3,000 copies printed were seized at the border. Orders for the arrest of Marx, Ruge, Heine and Bernays were issued, in case they returned to Prussia. In these circumstances, with lack of interest in France and the ban on its circulation in the Prussian-con-trolled territories, the journal had become unviable. The Zurich firm that had printed and published it lost interest. Ruge, who had invested a large sum of his own money, was not prepared to lose more of it. The first double number of the journal, as noted, was thus also its last.

There were also other reasons for the journal's inability to continue publication. Of these, the most important was the increasing ideological distance between the two editors that had gradually emerged over the period between the decision to publish the journal and its publication. The friendship between Ruge and Marx had developed during Marx's Young Hegelian days. From the time when Marx started to correspond regularly with Ruge until his resignation from the *Rheinische Zeitung*, Marx had, to put it broadly, subscribed to views that did not appear to clash with those held by Ruge. However, from the summer of 1843, when Marx threw himself deeply into the study of history and the theory of the state, his ideas began to change in the direction of a more radical and militant politics. As suggested earlier, in Paris Marx's thinking moved rapidly towards communism and as Ruge detested communism – he thought communist ideas would 'lead to police state and slavery'[6] – a break in the relationship between the two was inevitable.

In fact, differences in their viewpoints had gradually begun to emerge as soon as they started, in the summer of 1843, to discuss the programme of the review. Ruge was highly sceptical about the prospects of political change in Prussia and saw the journal as more literary-philosophical in character, giving 'a calm but just and strict appraisal of the periodicals of the day' and publishing 'reviews of old-time writings and belles-lettres in Germany as well as reviews of books published in the two countries which open or continue the new epoch.' Marx wanted the journal's theoretical approach to be more directly related to the struggle against the Prussian absolutist state. In the event, Marx was able to modify the draft programme, at least in part, in line with his own thinking. Thus, for instance, the final version adopted read, in part: The journal will publish 'reviews of old-time writings and belles-lettres in Germany which of necessity will subject to criticism the old-time German spirit in its transcendent, now moribund existence …'[7]

The breach between Ruge and Marx was finally sealed after Marx's response to two articles by Ruge in the twice-weekly German language newspaper *Vorwärts!* published in Paris.

In these articles, published in July (1844), Ruge indulged in some tittle-tattle against the Prussian King and Queen, but also discussed some issues of social reform, particularly in the light of a recent uprising of weavers in Silesia. He referred to the uprising, during which workers had destroyed the newly installed machinery, and observed that the revolt was a futile protest of the poor, and without any particular significance. He wrote these articles under the pseudonym of 'A Prussian', though he was not a Prussian – he was member of the Dresden (Saxony) Town Council and as a foreigner in France, he was registered with the embassy of Saxony in Paris. Because of his close association with *Vorwärts!*, Marx, with some justification, thought that suspicion could fall on him as the author of the articles.

I will consider the content of Marx's article in the next chapter. Here it is sufficient to say that Ruge's remarks on the political situation in Germany evoked a fierce attack from Marx. Although Marx's article was essentially of a theoretical nature, its openly hostile tone ensured that the breach between the two friends would be final and complete. In concluding his article, Marx urged the 'super-clever Prussian' 'to refrain for the time being from all writing on political and social matters ... and instead sincerely to come to an understanding of his own condition.'[8]

Ruge was not the first friend with whom Marx had fallen out – it was Bruno Bauer – nor would he be the last. The reasons behind all such breaches were always political and ideological.

Life in Paris

The capital of France – at the time the world capital of socialism – provided Marx all the opportunities he needed to develop intellectually. During his stay in Paris he came to know all the leading French figures on the Left and became familiar with their theories. There were democratic socialists like Louis Blanc, Ledre-Rollin and Ferdinand Flocon, who believed in political reform through the democratic process based on universal suffrage. Such ideas appealed to many workers who had become disillusioned with revolutionary activity and insurrections that had ended in defeat.

Another school of thought was represented by Etienne Cabet, a utopian socialist who had been deeply influenced by the work of Sir Thomas More. His book *Journey to Icaria*, outlining a communist utopia, had had great success in France. A different line of thinking was represented by Pierre Leroux and P-J Proudhon, both of whom had risen from the ranks of workers. Proudhon's book *What is Property?* had answered the question with the answer 'Theft!' Marx befriended Proudhon and, by his own account, spent many friendly hours with him discussing Hegel. (Proudhon would be another friend that would later come under a passionate critical attack.)

There were other varieties of socialists such as Saint-Simonians and followers of Francois Marie Charles Fourier, and Christian socialists. What united them all was the belief that social reform would have to be achieved gradually – through the spread of education or the electoral process or the goodwill of the ruling classes.

It was also in Paris that Marx had his first contact with members of the working class. Paris had a large German emigré population, including a large number of artisans who had come to Paris either to seek employment or improve their skills, or because of political persecution in Germany. Many of them were organised in associations, some clandestine, others semi-clandestine. The most radical of these was the League of the Just (later to be reorganised as the Communist League). It had sister organisations in Zurich and London. The Paris branch was led by Hermann Ewerbeck, a medical doctor. He was under the influence of Cabet and had translated his *Journey to Icaria* into German.

Marx was greatly impressed by members of the League. His first impression of them he expressed in the following words:

> When communist artisans unite, at first doctrine, propaganda, etc., is the purpose of their meetings. But as they meet, they appropriate a new need, the need for society, and what appeared as a means now becomes an end. One can observe this practical movement in its most shining results, when one sees a meeting of socialist French workers. Smoking, drinking, eating, etc. are no longer there as means of connecting and as connecting means. Society, the association, the conversation, which, in turn, has society as its goal, suffices for them. The brotherhood of man is no phrase, but a truth to them and the nobility of humanity shines out at us from figures hardened by labour.[9]

Marx expressed similar sentiments in a letter to Feuerbach. Referring to his meetings with French workers, he wrote:

> It is a remarkable phenomenon that, in contrast to the 18th century, religiosity has now passed to the middle and upper classes while on the other hand irreligiosity – but an irreligiosity of men regarding themselves as men – has descended to the French proletariat. You have to attend one of the meetings of French workers to appreciate the pure freshness, the nobility which burst forth from these toil-worn men.[10]

This is an interesting letter, written on the 11 August. Marx by this time had become a communist, he had adopted the vision of a society without private property and the proletariat as the principal agent of social change. But at this point in time he believed that Feuerbach's philosophy could become the basis of a theory of socialism. He wrote to Feuerbach:

> Your *Philosophie der Zukunft,* and your *Wesen des Glaubens,* in spite of their small size, are certainly of greater weight than the whole of contemporary German literature put together.

> In these writings you have provided – I don't know whether intentionally – a philosophical basis for socialism and the Communists have immediately understood them in this way. The unity of man with man, which is based on real differences between men, the concept of the human species brought down

from the heaven of abstraction to the real earth, what is this but the concept of society![11]

We will see in a later chapter that between this time and the spring of 1845 he will have worked out his own philosophical basis of communism, which in the first instance would be developed as a critique of Feuerbach.

Marx's stay in Paris was a happy time for him. In May he became father of a little girl who was named Jenny, after her mother. The shareholders of the *Rheinische Zeitung* sent him a donation of a fairly large sum of money. The Marx household therefore had no financial worries. (Both husband and wife were generally indifferent to money matters.) Marx also enjoyed a rich social life. I mentioned earlier that he had befriended a number of socialist leaders. In particular, he enjoyed the company of the German poet Heinrich Heine. Heine, more than 20 years older than Marx, became a regular visitor to the Marx household.

Marx's daughter Eleanor in her memoirs recalled:

> He (Marx) loved the poet as much as his works and looked as generously as possible on his political weaknesses. Poets, he explained, were queer fish and they must be allowed to go their own ways. They should not be assessed by the measure of ordinary or even extra-ordinary men.[12]

Heine was a democrat and a mild kind of socialist and had no sympathy with communist ideas and 'the time when sombre iconoclasts will destroy my laurel groves and plant potatoes'.[13]

According to Eleanor, Marx was sorry to part with him when he had to leave Paris and both remained friends until Heine's death in 1856.

Marx was also friendly with another German poet, Georg Herwegh. Marx's idea that poets were exceptional people and should be judged by rules other than those appropriate to ordinary mortals applied to Herwegh as well. He was therefore tolerant of his sybaritic and philandering life style and this fact had provided another reason for the rift between him and Ruge who took a very different view of the self-indulgent mode of life of a married man. Another friendship that Marx formed at this time was with Michael Bakunin, a Russian aristocrat who later became famous as an anarchist thinker. This friendship was not to last long because of the strong political differences that developed between the two.

Meeting with Frederick Engels

Paris was also the venue for the meeting between Marx and Engels that resulted in their life-long friendship – friendship and collaboration that are unique in the annals of politics and scholarship. Two years younger than Marx, Engels had a very different family background from Marx's. His father, a strict pietist Christian, was a prosperous industrialist in Barmen in Rhineland. At the age of 18, after he had finished high school, young Frederick was sent to Bremen, north-west Germany, to work as an apprentice clerk in a commercial house. Three years later, he spent a year of military service in Berlin where he consorted with Young Hegelians and wrote for Ruge's *Deutsche Jahrbücher*. After he completed his military service in December 1842, his father sent him to England to work as a clerk in the Manchester textile factory Ermen and Engels of which he was part owner.

In Manchester Engels worked diligently and learned all the tricks of the trade but his heart did not lie in the 'damned business'. It lay in politics. He read widely in socialist and political economy literature, but, more importantly, working at the centre of English manufacturing he acquired first-hand knowledge of the working of British capitalism, at the time the most developed in the world. He also observed first-hand the dreadful living conditions of the working people associated with laissez-faire capitalism. Engels' *Deutsch-Französische Jahrbücher* articles thus captured many of the 'contradictions' of contemporary capitalism. As noted earlier, it was this new perspective in Engels' two articles that strongly impressed Marx whose intellectual development at that stage had largely come from his critique of Hegel. Fifteen years later, in his preface to *A Contribution to the Critique of Political Economy*, Marx referred to Engels' 'Outlines' article as a brilliant essay in the critique of political economy.

After spending 21 months in England, Engels, on his way from Manchester to Barmen, stopped in Paris and met Marx. They had met before in the office of the *Rheinische Zeitung* in the autumn of 1842. That meeting was a distinctly cool affair, as Marx associated Engels with the Young Hegelian 'Free Men' and their 'buffoonery' that he was finding intolerable. Now it was very different. Engels spent ten days in Paris and most of the time he was there he spent with Marx. By this time (late August-early September 1844) Marx had read a good deal of political economy – evidence of this reading is to be found in his *Economic and Philosophical Manuscripts of 1844*. What Engels brought to his discussions with Marx was his direct experience of the working of British capitalism. By now Engels had collected all the material for his *Condition of Working Class in England* that he would write in Barmen after leaving Paris and that would be published in Germany the following year.

Marx must have found Engels' account of the conditions in England extremely illuminating. Nearly 20 years later when Marx was composing his three volumes of *Capital* and struggling with such abstruse problems as the 'transformation of values into prices', he wrote to Engels (letter dated 9 April 1863), referring to Engels' book:

> What powers, what incisiveness and what passion drove you to work in those days. That was a time when you were never

worried by academic scholarly reservations! Those were the days when you made the reader feel that your theories would become facts if not tomorrow then at any rate one day after. Yet that very illusion gave the whole work a human warmth and touch of humour that makes our later writings – where 'black and white' have become 'grey and grey' – seem positively distasteful.[14]

Neither Marx nor Engels wrote about the ten days they spent together that laid the basis for a life-long friendship. The only account we have of their discussions in Paris is the one sentence Engels wrote two years after Marx's death (in 'On the History of the Communist League'):

> When I visited Marx in Paris in the summer of 1844, our complete agreement in all theoretical fields became evident and our joint work dates from that time.[15]

It was during these ten days that the decision to write their first joint work – *The Holy Family or Critique of Critical Criticism* – was taken. It was to be an attack on the recent writings of Marx's old friend Bruno Bauer, who along with his brothers Edgar and Egbert, was propagating a new 'worldview' in the journal *Allgemeine Literatur-Zeitung*. This was the view that no political progress in Germany could be made along the lines that had been adopted by the *Deutsch-Französische Jahrbücher* or the *Rheinische Zeitung*. In Germany no criticism of the absolutist monarchy was tolerated and 'the masses' were quite indifferent to the repressive policies of the government. Only philosophy and intellect ('critical criticism') will save Germany.

> To date great movements of history have been misguided and doomed to failure from the beginning because the masses interested themselves in them or were enthusiastically in favour of them; or they came to a miserable end because the idea around which they centred was one requiring no more than a superficial understanding, and reckoning therefore with the applause of the masses.[16]

The writings of the Bauer brothers at this time received little attention in Germany. According to Marx's first (and sympathetic) biographer, by the time Marx and Engels decided to respond to Bauer's new 'worldview' the entire Bauer project was 'not only dead but forgotten'.[17] Engels wrote his part – a modest contribution of 16 pages – and left for Barmen thinking that Marx would deal with the subject in the same dismissal fashion as he had done. He was surprised to find some months later that the proposed pamphlet had become a massive volume (300 pages) and felt it to be quite disproportionate to the 'supreme contempt we two evince towards the *Literatur-Zeitung*.'[18]

However, a short while later (10 May 1845), Engels put a slightly different gloss on the book. He wrote in the journal *New Moral World* that in Germany

> a war has been declared against those German philosophers who refuse to draw from their theories practical inferences, and who contend that man has nothing to do but speculate upon metaphysical questions. Marx and Engels have published a detailed refutation of the principles advanced by Bauer ...[19]

Marx himself, writing many years later (9 April 1867), also took a rather different view of the book. He wrote to Engels that on re-reading the book he was pleasantly surprised to find that they had no need to feel ashamed of the piece, although the Feuerbach cult now made a comical impression on him.

Though *The Holy Family* was essentially a polemical work, in writing his part Marx made significant advances in the development of his own world-view. The book went beyond anything he had written up to this point in emphasising the correspondence between politics and the economic structure of a country, observing that it was impossible to understand the history of any period 'without knowing ... the industry of that period, the immediate mode of production.'[20] (This point is fully discussed in chapter four, section 'The Beginnings of Historical Materialism'.)

The book was published in Frankfurt am Main in February 1845 and attracted some attention in Germany. The *Mannheimer Abend-Zeitung* referred to it as a 'profound and forceful work'; and the *Allgemeine Zeitung* attacked it for preaching revolt 'against the state, the church, the family, legality, religion and property.' It found the work all the more dangerous as

> Mr Marx cannot be denied either extremely broad knowledge or the ability to make use of the polemical arsenal of Hegel's logic, what is customarily called 'iron logic'.[21]

The Long Road to *Capital*: The Beginning

Sometime in January or February (1844) Marx must have thought that he now had enough material to publish a critique of Hegel's political philosophy. In the article 'Contribution to a Critique of Hegel's Philosophy of Law: Introduction' he declared his intention to complete the critique and have it published.[22] But the idea was soon abandoned. In the preface to *The Economic and Philosophical Manuscripts*, written over the months from April to August, he gave reasons for not having proceeded with this plan: 'While preparing it for publication, the intermingling of criticism directed only against speculation with criticism of the various subjects themselves proved utterly unsuitable, hampering the development of the argument and rendering comprehension difficult. Moreover, the wealth and diversity of the subject to be treated could have been compressed into one work only in a purely aphoristic style; whilst the aphoristic presentation of this kind, for its part, would have given the impression of arbitrary systematism'.[23]

He then goes on to say that he would instead write a series of distinct, independent pamphlets, presenting in each separate pamphlet subjects such as law, ethics, politics. He would then try to present these ideas in a single work, showing the interconnections of these separate parts, thus presenting an overall critique of idealist philosophy.

Marx did not proceed with this plan either. Instead he resumed the thread of his studies in the history of the French Revolution he had started in Kreuznach. He read widely in the subject and decided to write a book on the history of the Revolution. This plan of Marx's is confirmed by Ruge who wrote to Feuerbach in May (1844) reporting that Marx had suspended his work on Hegel's political philosophy and had instead decided to write a history of the Convention (the period between overthrow of the king in 1792 and the establishment of the directory in 1795). Ruge added that Marx was also going deeply into the study of French materialism. (Ruge also informed Feuerbach that Marx was working himself sick and at times did not go to bed for three nights in succession.) The plan to write this work was also reported by a radical newspaper in Marx's home town, Trier.[24]

Marx did not proceed with the writing of this book though his notes made at the time show his extensive reading on the subject.

Marx's studies in the history of the French Revolution coincided with his interest in the study of political economy. This was a major addition to his theoretical interests. During the spring and summer of 1844 he read widely in the subject. The range of his vast reading is shown in the notebooks he kept at the time. These are referred to as 'Paris Notebooks'. The notebooks contain excerpts made from different works, their summaries and Marx's own comments. The editors of his works at the Institute of Marxism-Leninism in Moscow extracted from these voluminous notes a certain amount of material that was given a systematic form and published for the first time, in German, in 1932. It was given the title *The Economic and Philosophical Manuscripts of 1844*. *The Manuscripts* are Marx's first attempt to synthesise his philosophical thinking with political economy. (This attempt at the synthesis of the two is discussed in chapter four).

Towards the end of the year (1844), after he had completed *The Holy Family*, Marx thought he had enough material to publish the results of his studies in a definitive form. To this end he signed a contract with a German publisher, Karl Leske, to write a book with the title *Critique of Politics and Political Economy*. Marx must have discussed this project with Engels during their August/September meetings because, in a letter dated 20 January

1845, Engels wrote to Marx:

> But what we require most of all is a couple of lengthy works, so that the many half-educated people who have the will, but not the means, to manage by themselves, can get a proper grasp of things. See if you can get your book on economics finished, even if you are not happy with it: it does not matter; the mood is right and we must strike while the iron is hot.[25]

Marx did not heed Engels' advice. He obviously thought he was not yet ready 'to launch his work in the world' as Engels had suggested. Leske continued to demand the delivery of the manuscript and Marx continued to give his reasons for the delay. Writing from Brussels (1 August, 1846), he wrote to Leske that it was important in order to prepare the public 'for my position on the *Economy* (by now he had dropped the word 'politics' from the title of the proposed book) to inform them of his criticism of German philosophy and German socialism. (This is a reference to the articles he wrote in Brussels criticising Bauer and others, including 'true German socialists'.) He also made reference to his six-week visit in the summer of 1845 to Manchester where he had devoted all his time to the study of political economy to gather 'new material for the book'. This necessitated revision of the 'first volume of my study' that had been 'lying here for so long'. He also informed Leske that a new two-volume work on the French political economy school of Physiocracy had just been published in Paris. 'Now they must be fully considered'.[26]

Losing all hope of receiving the manuscript, Leske cancelled the contract. We continue the story of Marx's *Economy*, briefly.

After his expulsion from France, Marx spent the next three years in Brussels. During this period Marx was able to fully develop his vision of the historical process which he (in collaboration with Engels) first presented in *The German Ideology* (1846) and then in *The Communist Manifesto*, published in February 1848. In this vision the transition from feudalism to capitalism in Europe was driven by economic development and the rise of a new class, the bourgeoisie. In this process a point had come when the institutions of the feudal society had become fetters on further progress. The feudal class was resistant to change, while the interest of the bourgeoisie lay in the development of new institutions appropriate to continuing development. It was this clash of class interests that had supplied the dynamic of economic and social development. Marx projected this model into the future, to the transition from capitalism to communism. The function of the *Economy*, as this work developed in Marx's mind, had now become to provide a theoretical schema that would give effect to this vision, that is, that will theoretically demonstrate the mechanics of the transition from capitalism to socialism.

After the revolutionary upheavals of 1848-49 (discussed in Chapter 5), having been expelled first from Germany and then from France and having settled in London, Marx resumed his work on his *Economy*. We get the first indication of this from a letter he wrote to Engels on 7 January 1851.[27] In this letter Marx raised with Engels a number of questions in Ricardo's theory of rent which show that he was going deeply into economic theory. Three months later (2 April) he thought he had made sufficient progress with his *Economy* to be able to write to Engels: 'I have got far enough to finish the whole crap in five weeks. And, when that is finished, I will write out *Economy* at home and launch myself into another science at the [British] Museum.'[28] The next day Engels sent his congratulations, saying he was glad that Marx had finished his *Economy*. But Marx was far – very far – from finishing his *Economy*.

Between this time and the winter of 1857 there is hardly any reference in his correspondence to matters relating to his *Economy*. Then, it seems, the economic crisis of 1857 spurred him to again start talking about the progress of his work. In a letter dated 18 December, he wrote to Engels: 'I am working stupendously ... writing the fundamentals of the *Economy* (that is quite necessary in order to let the public get to the bottom of the thing and help me as an individual to get rid of this nightmare.')[29] Three days later he reported to Ferdinand Lassalle that he was working on the 'fundamentals of the *Economy*,' adding:

> I am forced to spend the day ... working for my daily bread. So only the night remains for real work and then I am often disturbed by being unwell...[30]

Marx certainly had been working 'stupendously'. Since the publication of *The Communist Manifesto* he had written a large number of newspaper articles, he had published two pamphlets on the situation in France, *The Class Struggle in France* and *The Eighteenth Brumaire of Louis Bonaparte*, (in these publications he was using his materialist thinking to discuss current events) and at the time of this letter he was nearing the completion of his massive, 800-page *Grundrisse: Foundations of the Critique of Political Economy*, a work that may be considered as part of the preparatory material for the *Economy*.

From the beginning of 1858, Marx seems to have become acutely aware that over all these years he had published nothing of the much awaited 'critique of political economy'. (As early as 12 May 1851 Lassalle had written to him: 'I have heard that your *Economics* will at last see the light of day ... I am burning to contemplate on my desk the giant three-volume work of the Ricardo turned socialist and Hegel turned economist.'). In the letter to Engels of December 18 (1857), Marx proposed that 'we should put out a pamphlet together in spring (1858), as a re-announcement to the German public that we are still here, always the same.'[31] Nearly four months later (2 April 1858) he sent Engels the outline of his projected *Economy* consisting of six parts and suggested that the proposed work for immediate publication should deal with the first part only.

This part of the proposed work was published in 1859 under the title *A Contribution to the Critique of Political Economy*. As indicated, it contained only one small part of the projected work, and it did not tell a coherent story. Marx himself had written to Engels that although the book was meant to be on 'capital in general' it did not contain 'anything' on capital. (On first seeing the outline of the work, Engels had found the material 'very abstract, abstract indeed' and had followed the 'dialectical transitions only with difficulty.'[32]

The book, a highly abstract work, had a poor reception. Marx was devastated, He wrote to Lassalle:

> you are wrong if you think I expected much praise from the German press or even that I care a jot about it. I expected attack or criticism, but not a total silence.[33]

The material from this book was later incorporated into the first part of the first volume of *Capital*, arguably the densest and the least accessible part of this volume.

During the early 1860s, Marx completed the draft of the three-volume history of economic thought which was given the title *Theories of Surplus Value* (intended to be the fourth volume of *Capital*), and drafts of the second and third volumes of *Capital*. (All these, and *Grundrisse* remained unpublished during Marx's life.) With all these drafts lying before him he finally composed the first volume of his *Economics* on which he had started working 22 years earlier.

On 17 April 1867, he wrote to a correspondent:

> I travelled from London last Wednesday, by steamer, and reached Hamburg on Friday afternoon in a raging storm; I was there in order to deliver the manuscript of Volume I to Herr Meissner. Printing began at the beginning of the week, so that the first volume will appear at the end of May. The whole work is in three volumes. The title is: *Capital. A Critique of Political Economy*.[34]

Expulsion from France

From August (1844) Marx had started to take active interest in the German language newspaper *Vorwärts!*, referred to previously. The newspaper had been launched at the beginning of 1844 as a business venture by a German investor. Despite its moderate, liberal policy the Prussian government banned its circulation in Prussia.

The owner of the newspaper now appointed the radical journalist Bernays (who had contributed to the *Deutsch-Französische Jahrbücher*) as the new editor. The newspaper now began to adopt a more critical policy towards the Prussian government. Soon it became a meeting place for radical Germans such as Marx, Ruge, Heine, Herwegh, and Ewerbeck, leader of the League of the Just in Paris.

Marx first became a contributor and then joined the editorial board of the newspaper, practically directing its policy. Bitten by its criticism by the newspaper, and particularly the way it reported an unsuccessful attempt on the life of the King (the writer expressed the hope that the assassin will have better aim next time), the Prussian government made insistent demands on the French that the newspaper be closed down and that its leading lights be expelled from France.

After much hesitation the French government succumbed to Prussian pressure and ordered the newspaper to be closed down, and in January 1845 issued orders expelling Bernays, Marx, Ruge and Heine from France. The expulsion orders against Ruge and Heine were later rescinded. Marx was not so lucky. Soon after the order was issued, Marx (now 26 years old) left Paris for Brussels. After giving an undertaking not to write on current political affairs, he was allowed to stay in Belgium. His wife Jenny, with their eight-month daughter, followed him some days later.

NOTES

1 *MECW*, 3:142.
2 Ibid. pp.142-43.
3 McLellan, *Karl Marx – His Life and Thought*, p.62.
4 *MECW*, 3:134.
5 Ibid. pp.350-51
6 McLellan, p.99.
7 See 'Letters from *Deutsch-Französische Jahrbücher*', *MECW*, 3:133-145.
8 Ibid. p.206.
9 Quoted in Jonathan Sperber, *Karl Marx – A Nineteenth Century Life*, Liveright Publishing Corporation, New York, 2013, pp.148-49.
10 *MECW*, 3:355.
11 Ibid. p.354.
12 Quoted in Francis Wheen, *Karl Marx*, Fourth Estate, London, 1999, p.65.
13 David McLellan, p.103.
14 *MECW*, 41:466.
15 *MESW*, 2:344.
16 Quoted in Mehring, *Karl Marx, the Story of his Life*, p.98.
17 Ibid.
18 Quoted in Wheen, *Karl Marx*, pp.85-87. See also Engels' letter to Marx of 20 January 1845, in which he writes: 'That you enlarged the Critical Criticism to 20 printed sheets came of course as a surprise to me. But it is all to the good. Much has been available which would otherwise have remained locked up in your desk who knows how long.' Marx, Karl and Frederick Engels, *Marx-Engels Correspondence*, Progress Publishers, Moscow, 1975, pp.22-23.
19 *MECW*, 4:240-41.
20 Ibid. p.150.
21 Ibid. p.684.
22 *MECW*, 3:176.
23 Ibid. p.231.
24 Ibid. p.606
25 *Letters on Capital*, p.1.
26 Ibid. pp.3-4
27 Ibid., pp.17-20.
28 Ibid., p.27.
29 Ibid. p. 48.
30 Ibid. p.49.
31 Ibid.
32 Ibid. p.61.
33 Ibid. p.89.
34 Ibid. p.101.

3

A Critique of the Philosophical Expression of Capitalism*

A New Methodology

We have seen (Chapter 1) that Marx's view of the Hegelian idea of the state had gradually begun to change over the 10-month period that he spent with the *Rheinische Zeitung*. Writing in July 1842, he regarded the state as the great organism in which the individual realised his freedom and in which he obeyed the laws of the state as the laws of his own reason. The real, actual state he had considered as merely a deviation from the ideal, rational state. We also noted that during this period his thinking had begun to change. He was now making a clearer distinction between the rational state and the actual, 'political' state. The monograph *Contribution to the Critique of Hegel's Philosophy of Law* (the *Hegel Critique*) he wrote during the spring and summer of 1843 was a development of these doubts about Hegel's political philosophy.

It was also noted that Marx's interest in writing a critique of Hegel's political philosophy went back to March 1842 when he wrote to Arnold Ruge about his plan to write a critique of Hegel 'insofar as it concerns the *internal political system*'; and that despite repeated promises to send Ruge an article on the subject for publication, he was unable to deliver. It has been plausibly suggested that the delay in completing the critique was due to Marx not having an appropriate methodology to deal with the subject, and that this difficulty was resolved with the publication, in February 1843, of Ludwig Feuerbach's *Preliminary Theses on the Reform of Philosophy*.[1] The *Theses* made a powerful impact on Marx.[2]

Hegel's idealist philosophy had attempted to solve the traditional philosophical problem of dualism between mind and matter, thought and reality, by postulating that reality is merely a manifestation, projection of 'world spirit', in Marx's words man's process of thinking. In other words, reality is phenomenal, it has no independent existence. 'In the beginning' consciousness does not recognise that objects, the external world is merely a projection of itself.[3]

The process of historical development is the process of consciousness realising that all that appears external is in fact projection of itself; there are no objects outside consciousness. With this realisation, consciousness overcomes its alienation.

In his *Theses*, Feuerbach reversed the Hegelian relationship between consciousness and reality. Philosophy, he argued, should recognise the primacy of the senses; it should start with the real man and not world spirit or consciousness. He wrote: 'The relationship of thought to being is this: being is the subject, thought is predicate, thought proceeds from being, not being from thought.' Man is not an expression or attribute of God. On the contrary, God is the expression of the thought process of man. He wrote:

> Man – this is the mystery of religion – projects his being into objectivity, and then makes himself an object of this projected image of himself... Thus in God man has his own activity, an object. God is, *per se*, his relinquished self.[4]

This is the definition of man's self-alienation in the realm of religion.

This is the materialist standpoint arrived at through the inversion of Hegel's idealist philosophy that Marx needed to develop his own critique of Hegel's political philosophy. Marx extends this approach from religion to the political sphere. He wrote in the *Hegel Critique*:

> Just as it is not religion which creates man but man who creates religion, so it is not the constitution which creates the people but the people which creates the constitution.[5]

Marx's general approach to Hegel's philosophical thought from now will be that it contains truth but in 'mystified' form; that it presents many of the real processes in social life in an abstract, metaphysical form. One could arrive at the truth by de-mystifying Hegel.

The Problem of Dualism in Society
Hegel's political philosophy attempts to solve the problem of dualism in society. Marx adopted this problem as very much his own, though he interpreted the nature of the problem in terms different from Hegel's. And the solution to this problem – which Hegel, according to him, had failed to resolve – will become central to his thought.

The problem arose (as Marx saw it) with the transition from feudalism to capitalism and the emergence of the modern state. There were two aspects of this great transformation that Western Europe underwent from, say, around 1500. First, there was a fundamental change in the nature of property. According to Marx, in all earlier societies property had a social dimension; for instance, under feudalism landed property was not freely disposable, and the serf had rights on the property on which he worked. Under capitalism property received its purely economic form by discarding its former political and social associations, becoming free and disposable. This was private property in its 'pure' form.

Second, there arose, in institutional terms, a clear distinction between the state, the public domain, and the domain of private interest, what Hegel had referred to as 'civil society'. The state now became a distinct and differentiated organism from the economy; political rule became distant from the class structure of society. Such a distinction was absent in all earlier societies. Marx wrote in the *Hegel Critique:*

> In the Middle ages there were serfs, feudal estates, merchants and trade guilds, corporation of scholars, etc.; that is to say, in the Middle Ages property, trade, society, man are political ...every private sphere has a political character or is a political sphere... In the Middle Ages the political constitution is the constitution of private property, but only because the constitution of private property is a political constitution. In the Middle Ages the life of the nation and the life of the state are identical. Man is the actual principle of the state – unfree man. It is thus the democracy of unfreedom – estrangement carried to completion.

Marx emphasised this point again and again: in the Middle Ages the economy was embedded in the political and social life, political life and economic and social life were integrated.

> The estates of civil society and the estates in the political sense were identical, because civil society was political society – because the organic principle of civil society was the principle of the state.[6]

The problem for Hegel arose from the fact that modern capitalist society functions on the principle of individualism; that is, individuals pursue their private ends without regard to the interests of other members of society. And since under conditions of social division of labour and exchange, individuals must engage with each other, they are led to use others as means to their private ends. Civil society thus becomes (as he put it) the playground of competing interests which make for 'ethical degeneration'.[7]

Marx echoed this point (in the article 'On the Jewish Question' written immediately after the *Hegel Critique*):

> Where the political [actual] state has attained its true develop-
> ment, man – not only in thought, in consciousness, but in *real-*
> *ity*, in *life* – leads a two-fold life, a heavenly and an earthly life:
> life in the *political community*, in which he considers himself a
> *communal being* and life in *civil society*, in which he acts as a *pri-*
> *vate individual*, regards other men as means, degrades himself
> into a means, and becomes the plaything of alien powers.[8]

He referred to dualism as 'the conflict between the *general interest* and the *private interest*, schism between the *political state* and *civil society'*, and re-ferred to civil society as the sphere of egoism.

The other aspect of life, as mentioned, is represented by the state. In this sphere of their lives, people are united in a common bond, a bond of solidar-ity which makes them an organic whole, a community, a nation. In Hegel's conception, the community is the product of history. It has evolved over time as only an organism can; individuals are related to each other as parts of an organism.

> They are held together by the single life they share. The parts
> depend on the whole for their life, but on the other hand, the
> persistence of life necessitates the differentiation of the parts.[9]

In this aspect social life is governed by the principle of social solidarity (as opposed to civil society where it is governed by the principle of individual-ism). The state is a manifestation of the spiritual essence of the people; the world spirit is embodied in the state.

Hegel's idea of the state as an ethical entity required resolution of the problem of dualism. His theory had to recreate, *at a higher level of develop-ment*, the unity that characterised society before the economy became dif-ferentiated from the political sphere; it had to resolve the conflict between the state and civil society such that individuals lived by universal criteria, and the individualism or egoism that is the foundation of civil society was reined in. In other words, his theory has to achieve reconciliation between the general interest and the particular interest *in the state*, in the realm of social solidarity.

To better understand Hegel's (and Marx's) problem it will be helpful to recall that the dualism or 'schism' between political life and economic life that presented a challenge for him and to Marx was celebrated by the political economists of the 18th century – the time when the broad outlines of the capitalist economy had clearly emerged in parts of Europe. It became the principal task of classical political economy to conceptualise the new economy and theoretically demonstrate that it had a logic of its own, that it functioned without state interference; indeed it would function better when left alone; and, crucially, that there was no tension between the pursuit of individual self-interest and the general interest of society. In fact, political economy claimed that there existed a social mechanism that ensured that the general interest was best served when, in a framework of competitive markets, individuals were left free to pursue their egoistic impulses independently of the interests of others.

Admittedly, the state had a social function, but this role, in classical political economy, was confined to ensuring a framework of law and order in which individual freedom and property were protected, and to undertaking those socially necessary functions that individuals were unable to perform for themselves, acting individually. But private interest was seen to be prior to the general interest; reconciliation between the two took place *in the domain of private interest, in the competitive market*. It was in this manner that political economy presented a rationale of modern competitive capitalism.

Hegel's Solution to the Problem of Dualism

Hegel's model consists of a political and institutional structure that (he claims) corresponds to his ideal of the state.[10] It consists of hereditary, constitutional monarchy, the executive or the bureaucracy appointed by the monarch, the estate that devotes itself to the service of the government pursuing only the universal interest, and a two-chamber legislature. The upper house of the legislature is based on hereditary peerage (consisting of the class of landowners – 'the agricultural estate') and the lower chamber that is *indirectly* elected by civil society ('the business estate'). It is through the election of the lower chamber that the claimed reconciliation between the private and the general interest is achieved and the schism between the state and civil society overcome.

It is a fundamental premise of Hegel's theoretical system that the individual *qua* individual cannot be incorporated into the universality of the state. The individual is like an atom that cannot be directly absorbed in the collective. According to him an individual acquires personality only as member of a group or social order, an estate. He writes:

> When we say that a human being is 'somebody', we mean that he should belong to a specific estate, since to be a 'somebody' means to have substantial being. A person with no estate is a mere private person and does not enjoy actual universality.[11]

For Hegel, the agricultural estate does not present any problem. He refers to it as the 'immobile' part of society, and according to the medieval character of the estates system, landowners attend the legislature in person, rather than as elected delegates. The land belongs to the family and on the principle of primogeniture it is passed down the family through the eldest son; it is inalienable, that is, it lies outside the market. It is this fact – that historically the landed family is rooted in the soil – that gives the gentry its privileged position in society. It is organically part of society, and its interest coincides with the general interest.[12] It is the rest of civil society, characterised by moveable property that presents the problem. Individuals in this part of society are *atomistically* dispersed, lacking any 'political cohesion'.[13]

What this means is that there must be institutions that 'mediate' between the individual and the state. The mediating institution in the sphere of industry and trade is the corporation, each trade or industry having its own such association.

The corporation is a kind of 'second family' for its members.[14] Members of a corporation have common interests which are distinguished from those operating in other trades. The corporation will naturally look after these common interests. Members of a corporation will also have conflict of interest with each other. For instance, members compete with each other in the market.

Hegel does not go into such mundane detail but we may assume that it will be the task of the corporation to manage internal competition, say with respect to prices and output levels. The central claim here is that through the corporation individuals learn to give greater priority to their common interests over individual interests and thus develop a greater sense of social solidarity. The corporation may thus be regarded as the first stage in the incorporation of the individual in the state organism. Deputies from various corporations come together in an estate. This is the second stage of mediation. And finally, delegates from this estate (or the chamber), together with the estate representing the landowners, constitute the legislature.

This is how in Hegel's model, when it is brought down to earth from its metaphysical heights, the individualism and the conflicts of civil society are transcended, and the reconciliation of the private and public interest achieved. Civil society or the capitalist economy, which has now been purged of self-interest, retains its autonomy.

At the same time, the economy is overseen by a highly centralised state – it operates 'under the surveillance of the public authority',[15] with political power resting with the monarch and the bureaucracy. Hegel's is a corporatist capitalist economy in which competition is reined in. This may be seen as Hegel's response to the challenge of classical political economy that achieves the coincidence of the public and private interest through the competitive market.

To conclude: both models – Hegel's and political economy's – provide a rationale of the late 18th century and early 19th century capitalist economy, Hegel gives capitalism a *philosophical expression*, while classical political economy does it by constructing a *theoretical model* of a competitive economy. Marx's own thought will develop through a critique of both these approaches.

The *Hegel Critique*

In the *Hegel Critique*, Marx's discussion is focused on what he had earlier referred to as his 'internal political system', that is, on those parts of Hegel's *Philosophy of Right* that deal with constitutional arrangements (paragraphs 257 to 321). The central point in Marx's criticism of Hegel's constitutional arrangements is that the device purporting to mediate between the individual or civil society and the state fails to achieve the desired result, that is, to recreate the integrated unity that characterised the Middle Ages. The delegates that make up the business estate do not represent the general interest of society; rather, they attend to their own sectional interests. In any case, the real power rests with the estate of the bureaucracy which is responsible to the monarch. These arrangements are incapable of integrating the individual with the state. The individual remains alienated from the political process.

During the course of this criticism, Marx makes important advances in the development of his thought, and he takes the first step in the formation of his own definition of the ideal society, the 'rational state'.

First, Hegel's solution is based on a mystification; he solved the problem philosophically but was unable to relate this solution to the contemporary world. Hegel started with the ideal and then constructed a real-world political structure and claimed that it was in the image of the ideal. According to Marx, Hegel depicted the essence of the state *as in fact it is*, the actual state, but pretended that the state as it in fact is, is the essence of the 'genuine' or the 'rational' state. In other words, Hegel's mystification consisted in the fact that he deduced real world phenomenon from concepts, by making the real, empirical world reflection of the ideal, he made the abstract idea the determinant and reality the determined.

As noted earlier, although for Marx dualism was a problem that needed resolution his understanding of the nature of the problem differed from Hegel's. For Hegel the state is of the heaven and civil society of this world; hence the need for 'mediation'. For Marx the separation is mainly institutional. The economy has been dis-embedded from political life. In fact – and this is the first revolutionary conclusion – all the sectional interests of civil society powerfully influence the character of the state. And this leads to the conclusion that in order to understand the working of the political sphere you need to understand the working of civil society.

This is the method acquired in the *Hegel Critique* that from now on Marx will use in all his work.

The second major advance (related to the first) made by Marx refers to the nature of society. It was noted earlier that Marx had, following Hegel, adopted the notion of the organic nature of society; he had noted that a great merit of Hegel's philosophy was that it proceeded from 'the idea of the whole'. But Hegel's notion of society was metaphysical. He was not dealing with the real, empirical man. Here too the advance is made by inverting Hegel. Marx wrote: 'Hegel starts from the state and makes man the subjectified state; democracy [Marx's ideal political constitution] starts from man and makes state objectified man.'[16]

And again:

> This nonsense comes in because Hegel takes state functions and activities in abstract isolation, and the particular individuals in antithesis to them. He forgets, though, that the particular individual is human and that the functions and activities of the state are human functions. He forgets that the essence of a 'particular' personality is not its beard, its blood, its abstract physical character, but its *social quality*, and that state functions, etc., are nothing but modes of being and modes of action of the social qualities of men. Clearly, therefore, insofar as individuals are bearers of state functions and powers, they must be regarded in the light of their social and not their private quality.[17]

Marx argues that man must be conceptualised on an empirical plane, in his historical and social context. He kept coming back to this idea of the socialised model of man as opposed to the notion of the atomised society and Hegel's 'abstract' individual again and again. For instance, he wrote in the *Grundrisse*:

> Society does not consist of individuals; it expresses the sum of connections and relationships in which individuals find themselves. It is as though one were to say: from the stand-point of society there are neither slaves nor citizens: both are men... To be a slave or to be a citizen are social determinations, the relationships of Man A and Man B.[18]

In the *Hegel Critique* Marx is not attempting to define the features of his ideal state which here he refers to as the 'rational' or the 'genuine' state to distinguish it from the state that actually exists. But in his acceptance of dualism as a problem that needs resolution, that is, the overcoming of the distinction between the state and civil society, we may see the first intimation of the idea of the 'disappearance' of the state.

Critique of the Classical Liberal State

The article 'On the Jewish Question', written just as the *Hegel Critique* had been completed, is ostensibly a review of two articles by Bruno Bauer on the 'Jewish question' – the demand of German Jews that they be given the same rights as German Christians. Bauer had argued that to solve the 'Jewish question' Jews must first give up any claims based on religion, and then demand that the Prussian state give up its relation with religion. Once Christianity had lost its privileged position, that is, once the state had become secular, the 'Jewish problem' would simply disappear.

In this article, Marx continues his discussion of the issues raised in the *Hegel Critique*. He argues that 'political emancipation' (a secular, liberal state) would certainly be a step forward in a semi-feudal, autocratic country such as Prussia, but what political liberalism did was to sanctify the principle of individualism; the Rights of Man were the rights of an egoistic man. The right of man to private property is 'the right to enjoy one's property ... without regard to other men, independently of society, the right of self-interest.... It makes every man see in other men not the realisation of his own freedom, but the barrier to it.'[19] Marx is now talking of 'human emancipation', a social revolution.

The political state ensured universal rights of private property, equality of all citizens before the law, and freedom of conscience. The freedom of conscience meant the transfer of religion from the realm of politics to the private sphere, civil society. The state freed itself from religion, but the individual did not achieve freedom from religion. This demonstrated the limits of political emancipation.

According to Marx, the existence of religion in society even when exercised through 'free' choice is the existence of a defect in society. It is a self-imposed limitation on man. Free choice in this case is the choice of an unfree man. Man is alienated in the Feuerbachian sense: he can experience himself only by surrendering to something that is his own creation. Marx extends this idea – religious alienation – to political alienation. Man bestows his powers on the state, which is his own creation and which then comes to dominate him. To amend Feuerbach's aphorism, the state is man's relinquished self. 'Alienated man, (writes Marx)':

> acknowledges himself only in a roundabout route, only through an intermediary. Religion is precisely the recognition of man in a roundabout way, through an *intermediary*. The state is the intermediary between man and his freedom. Just as Christ is the intermediary to whom man transfers the burden of his divinity, all his burden of divinity, all his religious constraint [bonds], so the state is the intermediary to whom man transfers all his non-divinity and all his unconstraint [freedom].[20]

Marx here takes the first step towards his conception of man's alienation in the economic sphere, an idea he will develop fully a few months later in his *Economic and Philosophical Manuscripts of 1844*. He writes here:

Just as man, so long as he is engrossed in religion, can only

> objectify his nature by turning it into an *alien* creature of the fantasy, so, under the domination of egoistic need, he can act in a practical way, create objects practically, only by subordinating these products as well as his activity to the power of an alien being – money.[21]

Emancipation of Jews as well as of Christians can only be part of general human emancipation which will be achieved only when man has overcome his alienation in all spheres of life – religious, political and economic, that is, when society is so organised that it is free from the power of religion, the state, private property and money.

> Only when man has recognised and organised his *'forces propres'* [own powers] as social forces, and consequently no longer separates social power from himself in the shape of political power, only then will human emancipation have been accomplished.[22]

It was noted in the preceding chapter that at this time (the second half of 1843), when he was writing the *Hegel Critique* and 'On the Jewish Question', Marx had no idea that he was moving towards the idea of communism.

Proletariat as the Agent of Social Change

Marx wrote his 'Introduction' to the *Hegel Critique* about three months after he had completed the article 'On the Jewish Question'.[23] And in it he continued to develop his ideas articulated in these two papers. The style of the 'Introduction' is markedly different from the earlier articles. It has the elan, the dash that anticipates the style of *The Communist Manifesto*. Marx's thinking in this article is directed towards change; social criticism must lead to action to effect social change; and here he introduces his new idea that it will be the proletariat that will be the agent of change.

Marx opens the discussion with some remarks about religion that lead to the aphorism, religion is the opium of the people, quoted around the world countless times. According to Marx, in Germany criticism of religion had been completed. But this criticism had remained within the Feuerbachian anthropological frame, without leading to social criticism. Religion is man's inverted consciousness because the world that produces religion is an inverted world. Religion is the 'fantastic realisation' of the human world inasmuch as the human being possesses no true reality. The struggle against religion is, therefore, indirectly a struggle against the world whose spiritual aroma is religion. Now that the truth of man's self-alienation in the realm of religion has been revealed, it becomes the task of criticism to unmask man's self-alienation in all its forms.

It is in this context – unmasking of human alienation in its 'unholy', secular form – that Marx introduces the theme of the relationship between theory and practice – the idea that understanding the world and changing it are two aspects of the same process. You cannot detach thought from reality and consider it as a self-determining force. Marx writes:

> The weapon of criticism cannot, of course, replace criticism by weapons, material force must be overthrown by material force; but theory also becomes a material force as soon as it has gripped the masses. Theory is capable of gripping the masses as soon as it demonstrates *ad hominem,* and it demonstrates *ad hominem* as soon as it has become radical. To be radical is to grip things by the root. But for man the root is man himself. The evident proof of the radicalism of the German theory, and hence of its political energy, is that it proceeds from a resolute *positive* abolition of religion. The criticism of religion ends with the teaching that *man is the highest being for man,* hence with the *categorical imperative to overthrow all relations* in which man is a debased, enslaved, forsaken, despicable being ...[24]

Marx turns to the question of human emancipation of Germany, and this leads him to consider, for the first time, the question of the stages through which fundamental social change can be achieved. Must Germany go through a bourgeois revolution of the French type to reach the goal of human emancipation? German reality, Marx argues, has not risen to the 'intermediate stage' of political revolution experienced by modern European nations.

A political revolution requires social polarisation, on the one hand a class of oppression (such as the nobility and the clergy in France before the 1789 Revolution) and, on the other, a class (as the bourgeoisie in France) 'with an impulse of enthusiasm in itself' and that is capable of proclaiming its claims and rights as the claims and rights of society at large. But such a sharp distinction does not exist in Germany. Every class,

> once it begins the struggle against the class above it, is involved in the struggle against the class below it. Hence the princes are struggling against the monarchy, the bureaucracy against the nobility, and the bourgeoisie against them all, while the proletariat is already beginning to struggle against the bourgeoisie. No sooner does the middle class dare to think of emancipation from its own standpoint than the development of the conditions and the progress of political theory pronounces this standpoint antiquated or at least problematic.[25]

Marx will soon change his mind on this point: Germany will have to go through the 'intermediate stage', the bourgeois revolution before it can have a proletarian revolution. (See Chapter 5.)

Who will then lead the struggle to achieve human emancipation in Germany? By an interesting twist of logic, Marx argues that while in countries like France political emancipation (bourgeois revolution) can eventually lead to human emancipation, in Germany, which is unable to arrive at human emancipation through the intermediate stage of a political revolution, human, universal emancipation becomes 'the *conditio sine qua non* of any political emancipation'. Thus, German emancipation lies in the

> ... formation of a class with radical chains, a class of civil society which is not a class of civil society, an estate which is the dissolution of all estates, a sphere which has a universal character by its universal suffering and claims no particular right because no particular wrong but wrong generally is perpetrated against it; which can no longer invoke a historical but only a human title; which does not stand in any one-sided antithesis to the consequences but in an all-round antithesis to the premises of the German state; a sphere, finally, which cannot emancipate itself without emancipating itself from all other spheres of society and thereby emancipating all other spheres of society, which, in a word, is the complete loss of man and hence can win itself only through the complete rewinning of man. This dissolution of society as a particular estate is the proletariat.[26]

It is worth noting here that Marx arrives at the idea of the revolutionary role of the proletariat entirely through philosophical criticism. The proletariat is the general expression of man's alienation in a society characterised by the domination of private property; it carries within itself the same universal quality that Hegel had bestowed on bureaucracy, the universal class that had no interest other than that of society. The proletariat receives its universal character through sheer necessity, and the fact that it cannot free itself without freeing society as a whole.

Marx's article, 'Critical marginal notes on the article The King of Prussia and Social Reform: By a Prussian', as noted in the preceding chapter, was written as an attack on an article written by his former friend Arnold Ruge. In this article, published in August (1844) in a Paris newspaper, Marx articulates more clearly than he had done in his earlier articles his developing materialist method – the idea that the character of the state and politics, at any time, reflects the economic and social conditions prevailing at the time, and therefore politics is constrained by these economic conditions.

In his article Ruge had wondered, 'why does the King of Prussia not at once issue a decree for the education of all uncared for children?' Marx responds:

> Does the Prussian know what the King would have to decree? Nothing less than the *abolition of the proletariat*. In order to educate children they have to be *fed* and freed from wage-labour. The feeding and education of the uncared-for children, i.e., the feeding and education of the *entire rising generation* of the proletariat, would be the *abolition* of the proletariat and pauperism.[27]

Marx emphasises the point that the subjective will of the rulers is limited by the objective conditions prevailing in society. During the French Revolutionary period the Jacobin had attempted to force the will of the state on the socio-economic conditions of life; had thought that the subjective will of its leaders could achieve all it wanted, thus reducing political power to arbitrariness. He wrote:

> Thus, *Robespierre* saw in great poverty and wealth only an obstacle to *pure democracy*. Therefore he wished to establish a universal Spartan frugality. The principle of politics is the *will*. The more one-sided and, therefore, the more perfected the *political* mind is, the more does it believe in the *omnipotence* of the will, the more is it blind to the *natural* and spiritual *limits* of the will, and the more incapable is it therefore of discovering the source of social ills.[28]

Marx here repeats the view that a social revolution in Germany, led by the proletariat, could bypass the 'intermediate' stage of a political, bourgeois revolution. In Germany, the bourgeoisie is under-developed, and against this the proletariat has achieved a high degree of political consciousness. In support of this view he refers to the socialist writings of the journeyman tailor Wilhelm Weitling (whom he would castigate later) and the recent uprising of weavers in Silesia.

Always an over-optimist where prospects of revolution were concerned, Marx (who by this time had become a communist) saw in this uprising the growth of class consciousness of the proletariat, proclaiming its opposition to private property:

> The Silesian uprising *begins* precisely with what the French and English workers' uprisings *end*, with consciousness of the nature of the proletariat. The action itself bears the stamp of this *superior* character. Not only machines, these rivals of the workers, are destroyed, but also *ledgers*, the titles to property.

And he adds that the disparity between the political and philosophical development of the Germans is not an anomaly.

43

A philosophical people can find its corresponding practice only in socialism, hence it is only in the *proletariat* that it can find the dynamic element of its emancipation.[29]

I will conclude this chapter with the brief observation that although in the writings discussed in this chapter, Marx had assembled a number of elements that will form his developed materialist method, and that he had become a communist, he still did not have his own philosophical basis of communism. In a letter of 11 August (1844), the time when the *Critical Marginal Notes* article was published, he was writing to Feuerbach that the latter's philosophy could form the basis of communism. He will finally come out of the shadow of Feuerbach in the spring of 1845, with his *Theses on Feuerbach*.

NOTES

* Some of the material in this chapter and chapter four was first presented in a paper at the conference 'Marx 1818-2018 – New Developments on Karl Marx's Thought and Writings' held in Lyon, France, from 27 September to 29 September, 2017. In a modified form it has been published under the title 'Marx – From Hegel and Feuerbach to Adam Smith: A New Synthesis' in *International Critical Thought*, vol. 8, no. 2, June 2018.

1 See Robert C. Tucker, *Philosophy and Myth in Karl Marx*, Cambridge University Press, London,1961, pp.96-97, also Shlomo Avineri, *The Social and Political Thought of Karl Marx*, Cambridge University Press, London,1975, pp.9-10.

2 *MECW*, 1:400.

3 Historical evolution in Hegel does not take place in time, only in logic.

4 Quoted in Tucker, p.87.

5 *MECW*, 3:29.

6 Ibid. p.72, see also p.82.

7 G.W.F. Hegel, *Outlines of the Philosophy of Right* (translated by T.M. Knox) Oxford University Press, Oxford, 2008, p.182.

8 *MECW*, 3:154-55.

9 Editor's note in Hegel's *Outlines of the Philosophy of Right*, p.336.

10 It is important to note that according to Hegel his model presents in an idealised form features of the real world (developed, Protestant Europe) that have already been realised. Philosophy, according to him, comes only after the event. 'The owl of Minerva begins its flight only with the falling of the dusk.' *Outlines of the Philosophy of Right*, p.16.

11 Ibid. p.197.

12 Hegel writes: 'This estate is more particularly fitted for political position and significance in that its resources are independent alike of the state's resources, the uncertainty of business, the quest for profit, and any sort of fluctuation in possessions. It is likewise independent of favour, whether from the executive or the masses. It is even fortified against its own arbitrary will, because .... it is 'burdened with primogeniture'. Ibid., pp. 292-93.

13 Ibid. p.294-95.

14 Ibid. p.226.

15 Ibid. p.224.

16 *MECW*, 3:29

17 Ibid. pp.21-22.

18 David McLellan, *Marx's Grundrisse*, Paladin, St. Albans, Herts., 1973, p.89.

19 *MECW*, 3:163.

20 Ibid. p.152.

21 Ibid. p.171.

22 Ibid. p.168.

23 'Contribution to the Critique of Hegel's Philosophy of Law: Introduction'. This article, with 'On the Jewish Question' was published in the *Deutsch-Französische Jahrbücher* in February 1844.

24 *MECW*, 3:182.

25 Ibid. p.185-86.

26 Ibid. p.186. .

27 Ibid. pp.196-97.

28 Ibid. p.199.

29 Ibid. p.202.

4

First Confrontation with Political Economy – A New Synthesis

Introduction

As we have seen in the preceding chapter, between the spring of 1843 and February 1844 Marx had worked out some of the most important components of his worldview. He was now a materialist. He had rejected Hegel's rationalisation of capitalism, private property and constitutional arrangements prevailing in the advanced capitalist countries such as France, Britain and the Netherlands, and he had identified the agency that would lead the social revolution that he was advocating. He had also formed some idea of what an ideal society would be: it would be one without the right to own private property and one in which the state and civil society would have been re-integrated. He had arrived at this standpoint solely through philosophical critique. It was at this point – when he was not yet 26 years old – that he turned to the study of political economy. As already noted, he made extensive notes on what he read. From these notes the set that related particularly to political economy was extracted by the editors of his works and, in 1932, published under the title *The Economic and Philosophical Manuscripts of 1844*.

Although Marx studied the works of a large number of economists, the author with whom he engaged most deeply was Adam Smith. It was with reference to Smith's work that he exclaimed: 'Political economy has merely formulated the laws of alienated labour.'[1]

In the course of this confrontation Marx made two major advances in the development of his thought. First, he takes a decisive step in the formulation of his own version of materialism, rejecting thereby all 'previous' materialism, including Feuerbach's. Second, he integrates Smith's conceptualisation of capitalism and its mode of operation with the philosophical standpoint he had developed up to this point. We see here also the beginning of Marx's theoretical critique of classical political economy.

We note here something of a paradox. How come that the founder of a worldwide movement against capitalism should find his source of inspiration in the work of the most respected prophet of capitalism? The paradox is soon resolved when we observe that there are two methodologically distinct aspects of Adam Smith's thought which he treated as one. One aspect relates to his social philosophy which is individualistic in character. This aspect seeks to provide a rationale of competitive capitalism. The other aspect is theoretical and scientific in which he treats an objective phenomenon – the nature and causes of the wealth of nations under condition of capitalist production. Marx had already, before his encounter with political economy, rejected the kind of social philosophy embodied in the first aspect of Smith's thought. It was the second aspect that provided Marx with his own source of analysis of capitalism and which he synthesised with his philosophical standpoint. And, further, it was in the discussion of this aspect that he took a decisive step in the formation of his own version of materialism.

The following section outlines, briefly, the social philosophy of Adam Smith. The three sections that follow this section discuss the manner in which Marx drew on the scientific aspect of Smith's *Wealth of Nations*, and in which he developed his own standpoint.

Adam Smith's Social Philosophy

In his social philosophy, Smith adopts the principle of individualism. Society is seen essentially in terms of exchange, a phenomenon that is the result of a 'natural propensity' in human beings. He believed that 'all members of human society stand in need of each others assistance'; and that society flourishes when 'the necessary assistance is reciprocally afforded from love'. But when this is not possible

> society may subsist among different men, as among different merchants, from a sense of utility, without any mutual love or affection; and though no man in it should owe any obligation, or bound in gratitude to any other, it may still be upheld by a mercenary exchange of good offices according to an agreed valuations.[2]

Smith appears to subscribe to the social contract theory in which society is seen as a voluntary organisation. In the quotation above, he sees society as a market.

The essential point underlying Smith's thought here is exchange, man's 'natural propensity' to 'truck and barter'. All economic phenomena follow from this. For instance, the phenomenon of division of labour is the result of this propensity. He writes:

> It [division of labour] is the necessary, though very slow and gradual consequence of a certain propensity in human nature which has in view no such extensive utility; the propensity to truck, barter, and exchange one thing for another.[3]

In the same vein, he traces the origin of money to this propensity.[4]

We note here also the idea of the immutability of human nature – the assumption of 'abstract man', without any historical and social conditioning. 'The uniform, constant, and uninterrupted effort of every man to better his condition, the principle from which publick and national, as well as private opulence is originally derived'[5] seems to be the driving force for capital accumulation and economic development. One can take the view that at least in this aspect of his thought, Smith seems to take the view that historical development, say, the transition from feudalism to capitalism, was the result of the working of this 'natural propensity' – the desire of every man to improve his condition led to the victory of capitalism over the artificial restrictions that governments had placed on it.

Finally, we have Smith' scientific theorem: The operation of competitive markets, that is, free mobility of capital and labour across different economic activities, will lead to a state of 'natural balance' (general equilibrium) of the economy. '

> The natural price ... is ... the central price to which all prices of all commodities are continually gravitating... But whatever may be the obstacles which hinder them from settling in this center of repose and continuance, they are constantly tending towards it.[6]

But to provide a rationale of capitalism, Smith goes beyond this scientific proposition. He claims that this situation of unhindered resource mobility leads not only to the 'natural balance' of the economy, but also to the coincidence of private interest and the general interest. That is, the individual while pursuing his own interest also at the same time is led by an invisible hand to promote the general interest of society.[7] This latter proposition is derived entirely pragmatically: there is no theoretical basis for it. His reasoning seems to run on the following lines: in a competitive market producers will be free, and choose, to invest in lines of production that offer them the highest profits, and workers will seek employment in industries and firms where they find the highest rewards for their abilities and skills. In these circumstances the wealth of the nation would be maximised, and the conditions for economic progress would be the most conducive. Smith then associates the increasing wealth of the nation with increasing general prosperity, and the latter with the general interest of society, or the coincidence of the general interest and private interest. The coincidence of the two takes place in the competitive market.

Adam Smith as the Martin Luther of Political Economy

The very first sentence of *The Wealth of Nations* reads:

> The annual labour of every nation is the fund which origi-
> nally supplies it with all the necessaries and conveniences of
> life which it annually consumes, and which consists always,
> either in the immediate product of that labour, or in what is
> purchased with that produce from other nations.

Marx did not read this sentence as a mere rhetorical flourish. He observed that Smith's political economy had acknowledged labour as its principle. He wrote:

> To this enlightened political economy, which has discovered
> – within private property – the subjective essence of wealth,
> the adherents of the monetary and mercantile system, who
> look upon private property only as an objective substance con-
> fronting men, seem therefore to be fetishists, Catholics. Engels
> was therefore right to call Adam Smith the Luther of Politi-
> cal Economy. Just as Luther recognised religion – faith – as the
> substance of the external world and in consequence stood op-
> posed to Catholic paganism – just as he superseded external
> religiosity by making religiosity the inner substance of man –
> just as he negated the priests outside the layman because he
> transplanted the priest into layman's heart, just so with wealth:
> wealth as something outside man and independent of him,
> and therefore as something to be maintained and asserted only
> in an external fashion is done away with; that is , this external,
> mindless objectivity of wealth is done away with, with private
> property being incorporated in man himself and with him be-
> ing recognised as its essence.[8]

Marx sees Smith as conceiving wealth as materialised labour. This idea which will appear in a more general form – extending it to all reality – in the first thesis on Feuerbach is the first clear and definite intimation of Marx's own version of materialism. In the first thesis Marx rejected all 'previous' materialism, including Feuerbach's. Previous materialism accepted the du-ality of matter and mind and gave primacy to matter. Reality was some-thing 'external', objective, given, and mind (for Marx this meant man) was conceived as passive. This is the crucial point. This is how (as Marx sees it) mercantilists conceived wealth, as something 'external' to man. Smith, by saying that it is nothing but materialised labour, did away with this 'mindless objectivity of wealth'. Marx is here rejecting the duality of man (mind) and reality. The idea that wealth is objectified labour is extended to all reality.

In *The German Ideology* (written with Engels) this idea is elaborated when Marx distinguishes between 'original' nature and 'historical' nature (that is, 'nature' made by man).

> He [Feuerbach] does not see that the sensuous world around him is not a thing given direct from eternity, remaining ever the same, but the product of industry and of the society; and, indeed [a product] in the sense that it is a historical product, the result of activity of a whole succession of generations, each standing on the shoulders of the preceding one, developing its industry and its intercourse, and modifying its social system according to the changed needs. Even the objects of the simplest 'sensuous certainty' are given him through social development, industry and commercial intercourse. The cherry tree, like almost all fruit trees, was, as is well known, only a few centuries ago transplanted by commerce into our zone, and therefore only by this action of a definite society in a definite age has it become 'sensuous certainty' for Feuerbach.[9]

Marx emphasises this point again and again. If man's activity were interrupted only for a year we would not only find an enormous change in the natural world, we would find the very existence of mankind threatened.

The point Marx is making is that if man creates the reality (historical nature) in which he lives, he can also change it. This is the activist element that Marx incorporated into his own version of materialism which he referred to as 'practical', 'historical', and 'communist'. The basis for this standpoint was clearly laid down when he referred to Smith as the Luther of political economy.[10] (For further discussion of this point see the first section of Chapter 6.)

Conceptualisation of Capitalism

Built into Smith's concept of wealth is the notion of economic reproduction, a process that takes place in real time. This year's cycle of production starts with the inputs, including labour's subsistence, inherited from the preceding year; these inputs are used up in the current year's production and are reproduced (with a surplus) and used in the following year. When part of the surplus is re-invested we have economic expansion. Marx could not have failed to see here the Hegelian notion of evolution. It is a situation of internally generated development or expanded self-reproduction without the involvement of any extraneous factor.

The concept of reproduction is central to Marx's theory of historical development. According to *The German Ideology*:

> History is nothing but the succession of the separate generations, each of which uses the materials, capital funds, the productive forces handed down to it by all the preceding generations, and thus, on the one hand, continues the traditional activity in completely changed circumstances, and on the other, modifies the old circumstances with a completely changed activity.[11]

Further, Adam Smith sees the production of wealth as a social activity, a collective enterprise. It takes the form of social division of labour. Different productive activities complement each other and are thus 'necessary to the existence of each other'.[12] In the very first chapter of *The Wealth of Nations*, Smith illustrates this phenomenon with reference to the manufacture of a day-labourer's woollen coat.

> Observe the accommodation of the most common artificer or day-labourer in a civilized and thriving country and you will perceive that the number of people whose industry a part, though but a small part, has been employed in procuring him this accommodation, exceeds all computation.

From the raising of the sheep, etc. to sorting, combing, spinning, weaving, transportation of the materials, the manufacture of tools and machinery for use in these activities, and so on and on, all these activities are involved in the production of this item which becomes *'the produce of the joint labour of a great multitude of workmen'*.[Emphasis added][13]

Individual labour has become social labour and the product satisfies a trans-subjective need.

The features of an economy outlined above are of a general nature; to various degrees they hold practically for all forms of human society. For example, all societies are characterised by social division of labour and of course they all reproduce themselves over time (if they did not they would cease to exist). Such features of an economy may be considered of a technical nature.

Adam Smith's analysis of the conditions under which the wealth of a nation expands is set specifically in the social organisation he calls 'the commercial society', that is, modern capitalism. It is specially his conceptualisation of such an economy with the specific purpose of investigating the factors that lie behind economic development that determines the structure of classical political economy and gives it its scientific character. It is this analysis that makes an important contribution to the social theory that Marx will develop later.

In Smith's model the 'commercial society' is divided into three social classes. These are defined in terms of the nature of the resources they own and their place in the production system. Landowners have no productive function and they derive their income – rent of land – from a resource (land) that is naturally scarce, in the sense that (unlike capital goods and labour skills) it is not reproducible. There are suggestions in his discussion of rent that there is conflict of interest between the landed class and the capitalist class (and society, more generally) – suggestions that Ricardo will later develop with the utmost rigour.

The central relation in the production system is that between the capitalist class and labour. The capitalist class consists of those who have accumulated capital (in the form of purchasing power) and who will 'naturally employ it in setting to work industrious people, whom they will supply with materials and subsistence, in order to make a profit by the sale of their work'.[14] Workers, as a class do not own capital and means of their subsistence and therefore they 'stand in need of a master to advance them the materials of their work, and their subsistence and maintenance till it [the product] be compleated.'[15]

The relationship between the two classes is one of power and latent antagonism. For the capitalist labour's wages are a cost like any other, say, feed for farm animals. Higher costs mean lower profits and the capitalist must therefore strive to have wages as low as possible. Workers, on the other hand, want their wages to be as high as possible. We have here two parties 'whose interests are by no means the same. The workmen desire to get as much, the masters to give as little as possible. The former are disposed to combine in order to raise, the latter in order to lower the wages of labour.' Smith adds: 'It is not, however, difficult to foresee which of the two parties must, upon all ordinary occasions, have the advantage in the dispute, and force the other into a compliance with their terms.'[16]

Smith then goes on to enumerate all the factors that work in favour of the masters. The only factor that works in favour of the workers is capital accumulation and economic expansion. Under these conditions when national prosperity is on the rise, and the demand for labour is buoyant, wages can rise above the level that is 'consistent with common humanity'.[17] However, although in this situation the conflict between capital and labour may be kept under check, the fundamental fact of the relationship of power and latent antagonism between the two classes remains unchanged.

On reading *The Wealth of Nations*, Marx must have thought that Adam Smith had already loaded the gun for him.

Generalisation of the Concept of Alienation

The most important accomplishment of the *Manuscripts* is the generalisation of the concept of alienation. Until now Marx had been, as noted, exclusively ploughing the philosophical field. Economic alienation now takes centre stage and this concept is now expressed in the capital-labour relation, in production.

The first form of economic alienation Marx identified is the alienation of the worker from his product. This form of alienation – 'a fact of political economy'[18] – is derived fundamentally from the capital-labour relationship as found in Smith. Marx's starting point is Smith's statement that all wealth, consisting of commodities, is produced by labour. Just as the religious man had 'objectified' or 'externalised' himself in the gods; just as the state was the 'externalisation' of man in the form of political power; in the same way labour 'objectifies' or 'externalises' itself in its product. Capital, since it consists of produced commodities, is also produced by labour, it is accumulated labour. Capital (Marx quotes Smith) is a certain quantity of labour stocked and stored up to be employed'; and again:

> The person who [either acquires, or] succeeds to a great fortune, does not necessarily [acquire, or] succeed to any political power [...] The power which that possession immediately and directly conveys to him, is the power of purchasing; a certain command over the labour, over all the produce of labour, which is in the market.

Marx concludes: 'Capital is thus the governing power over labour and its products.'[19]

In the very first paragraph of the 'First Manuscript', Marx paraphrases some of the observations from the chapter 'Of the Wages of Labour' in *The Wealth of Nations*, highlighting the relationship of power between capital and labour and the capitalist's ability to appropriate labour's product. 'His own labour as another man's property and that the means of his existence and activity are increasingly concentrated in the hands of the capitalist.'

> All these consequences are implied in the statement that the worker is related to the product of his labour as to an alien object... The alienation of the worker in his product means not only that his labour becomes an object, an external existence, but that it exists outside him, independently, as something alien to him, and that it becomes a power on its own confronting him. It means that the life which he has conferred on the object confronts him as something hostile and alien.[20]

To repeat: through its social power, capital, itself the product of labour, is able to appropriate labour's product; labour's own creation becomes a power over it. This is labour's alienation from its product.

The second form of alienation manifests itself in the act of production, 'in the labour process'.[21] The product from which the worker is alienated is but the result of his productive activity. 'How could the worker (Marx asks) come to face the product of his activity as a stranger, were it not that in the very act of production he was estranging himself from himself? The product is after all but the summary of the activity of production.'[22]

Marx starts from the premise that productive activity is an aspect of man's 'essence'.[23] His need to engage in productive activity goes beyond the need merely to maintain his physical existence. It is through 'conscious life activity' that man asserts his humanity, his 'species character'. Labour performed for the capitalist is labour solely aimed at physical existence; it is external to man's intrinsic need. It is a case of self-estrangement.

When man is estranged from himself, he is necessarily estranged from other human beings. This follows from the standpoint that man's 'species character' is essentially social. As already noted, for Marx society is nothing but the sum of the relationships in which individuals find themselves. Here he writes:

> The estrangement of man, in fact every relationship in which man [stands] to himself, is realised and expressed only in the relationship in which man stands to other men.[24]

We see here Marx moving towards what is perhaps the most momentous theoretical achievement in the development of his synthesis between his philosophical standpoint and the scientific discipline of classical political economy.

> Hence within the relationship of estranged labour each man views the other in accordance with the standard and the relationship in which man finds himself as a worker [*as a producer*]. (Emphasis added).[25]

Before his encounter with classical political economy (as noted earlier) the proletariat's role in 'human emancipation' was vaguely and un-empirically attributed to its 'universal suffering' and 'sheer necessity'. Now he speaks of the relationship of the worker to other workers and workers' relationship with capital in the context of production. This is the critical point of transition; before he spoke vaguely of the 'power of money', now he talks of the 'wage-system'[26] and identifies it with the system of private property; the abolition of one, he says, implies the abolition of the other. It is only when the wage-system is abolished that 'universal emancipation' will be achieved. He writes:

> From the relationship of estranged labour to private property it follows further that the emancipation of society from private

property, etc., from servitude, is expressed in the *political* form of the *emancipation of the workers*; not that *their* emancipation alone is at stake, but because the emancipation of the workers contains universal human emancipation – and it contains this, *because the whole of human servitude is involved in the relation of the worker to production, and all relations of servitude are but modifications and consequences of this relation.*[27] [Emphasis added.]

The source of all forms of alienation and man's powerlessness are to be found in the relations that arise in the process of production. Material relations determine all other relations.

The Beginning of the Critique of Political Economy

Thanks to his study of political economy, Marx now sees the alienated man under capitalism as a commodity, bought and sold in the market, and which (as noted) for the capitalist is merely an item of cost of production. Adam Smith, while discussing the level below which capitalists ('who generally have the advantage') could not reduce the 'ordinary wages even of the lowest species of labour', had referred to a 'computation' of Richard Cantillon's. According to this computation the minimum subsistence wage was that that was necessary to bring up a family and perpetuate 'the race of such workmen'. [28] Marx noted this notion on the very first page of the 'First Manuscript'. He observes:

> For it [political economy], therefore, the worker's needs are but the one need – to maintain him whilst he is working and insofar as may be necessary to prevent the race of labourers from [dying] out. The wages of labour have thus exactly the same significance as the maintenance and servicing of any other productive instrument, or as the consumption of capital in general required for its reproduction with interest, like the oil which is applied to wheels to keep them turning.[29]

Smith had seen the 'principle of natural liberty' in terms of the free mobility of resources in the economy: the freedom of the capitalist to invest and sell wherever his private interest led him, and the freedom of the worker to choose his occupation and employer. Marx points to the relation between capital and labour and their respective 'freedoms', and quotes a French observer of the contemporary scene in Britain:

> The worker is not at all in the position of a free seller vis-à-vis the one who employs him… The capitalist is always free to employ labour, and the worker always forced to sell it. The value of labour is completely destroyed if it is not sold every instant.

> Labour can neither be accumulated nor even be saved, unlike true [commodities].[30]

In Smith's system, economic development remains strictly within the frame of competitive capitalist relations. Marx took this to mean that in classical political economy the capitalist system was considered to be eternal. This view of the permanence of the capitalist system may be compared with Smith's own understanding of historical development before the emergence of capitalism.

In chapters 2 and 3 of Book three and chapter 1 of Book five of *The Wealth of Nations*, Smith traced human progress through four distinct stages identified as socio-economic organisational forms. The earliest form was based on hunting and food gathering, then came the society of shepherds (this is when private property first appeared); this was followed by the feudal society, which gave way to the contemporary commercial society. It seemed that with capitalism, history had come to an end. Smith was taking the existing property relations as a given datum, not only for analysing the working of the capitalist economy (which was legitimate and necessary), but also for understanding historical development. This is how Marx saw it.

Marx's own mature theory of capitalist development, by contrast to the Smithian schema, will attempt to show that there are forces inherent in the logic of the capitalist economy that will drive its evolution beyond the bourgeois horizon set for it by classical political economy. He will reach this result through an internal critique of the classical theory.

In the *Manuscripts*, Marx does not discuss the developmental aspects of the classical theory. (He will do it three years later in *The Poverty of Philosophy*.) But he does make an important discovery that will provide one of the important ingredients of his mature theory of capitalist evolution. This observation refers to the concentration of capital in fewer and fewer hands as a necessary aspect of capital accumulation. Marx sees that the Smithian competition is dynamic and has the tendency to undermine the competitive character of capitalism.

Marx takes up this point in the section entitled 'The accumulation of capitals and the competition among the capitalists'. Here Marx quotes extensively from *The Wealth of Nations* (also from other writers). Of particular interest is the quotation from the 'Introduction' to Book two of *The Wealth of Nations* where Smith discusses the relationship between capital accumulation, increase in the division of labour (in the plant) and increase in labour productivity. Implicit in this relationship is the phenomenon of economies of scale. Marx recounts the numerous advantages that larger enterprises enjoy over smaller ones. In a competitive environment some enterprises will manage to get bigger and then, because of the advantages of size they enjoy, will begin to 'squeeze' the smaller ones out of the market. This is how, concentration of capital in fewer hands takes place.[31]

> Accumulation, where private property prevails, is the concentration of capital in the hands of a few, it is in general an inevitable consequence if capital is left to follow its natural course, and it is precisely through competition that the way is cleared for this natural disposition of capital.[32]

The competitive character of capitalism is undermined through its own internal development.

With the concentration of capital, both in individual enterprises and regions comes, necessarily, the concentrations of labour, which, in turn, is a necessary condition for the development of working people's class consciousness. As noted, these considerations, leading to the conviction that the ingredients for the transformation of capitalism lie within its own manner of functioning, its inherent logic, will come later in the development of Marx's thought.

Beginnings of Historical Materialism

As noted in the second chapter, at their meetings in Paris towards the end of August (1844), Marx and Engels decided to write a joint work attacking the Young Hegelians who had abandoned their earlier radical views and were now adopting idealist and Right-wing positions. Engels wrote his part, a short contribution, while still in Paris and expected Marx to write something of a similar size. Marx, however, drawing on his earlier writings (including the *Manuscripts*) and studies in the history of the French Revolution, wrote a massive work, which was published in February the following year with the title *The Holy Family or Critique of Critical Criticism – Against Bruno Bauer and Company*. The book was an attack on the standpoint of Bruno Bauer and his Young Hegelian followers which claimed that theoretical activity was the only dynamic force in history. It was in the course of these polemical writings that Marx took his first significant step in the transition to historical materialism.

There are three considerations here that need to be highlighted. First, Marx observes that it is impossible to understand the history of a period without understanding the state of material production in that period; second, he clearly introduces the dialectical method in the understanding of history; and third, there is an emphatic expression of the leading role of the proletariat in understanding modern development, a role that arises from the conditions of material production. He writes:

> Of course, spiritualistic, theological Critical Criticism only knows (at least it imagines it knows) the main political, literary and theological acts of history. Just as it separates history from the senses, the soul from the body and itself from the world, it separates history from the natural science and industry and

sees the origin of history not in vulgar material production on the earth but in the vaporous clouds in the heavens.[33]

This is how he introduces the dialectical method in the understanding of modern historical development and highlights the leading role of the proletariat: Private property and the proletariat make up an antithesis, two sides of a contradiction; private property is compelled to maintain itself, and thereby its opposite in existence. Private property is the positive side of the antithesis, it wants to maintain the situation as it is. On the contrary, the proletariat, the negative side, is compelled by the contradiction between its 'human nature' and its conditions of life to abolish itself and thereby its opposite, private property.

> Indeed private property drives itself in its economic movement towards dissolution, but only through a development which does not depend on it, which is unconscious and which takes place against the will of private property by the very nature of things, only inasmuch as it produces the proletariat as proletariat, poverty which is conscious of its spiritual and physical poverty...[34]

He adds:

> It is not a question of what this or that proletarian, or even the whole proletariat, at the moment regards as its aim. It is question of what the proletariat is, and what in accordance with this being, it will historically be compelled to do. Its aim and historical action is visibly and irrevocably foreshadowed in its own life situation as well as in the whole organisation of bourgeois society today.[35]

The dialectical process that drives change is rooted in class activity, in the process of production.

Marx completed the writing of *The Holy Family* towards the end of November (1844). It will take him another five months to assemble all the elements of his worldview.

NOTES

1   *MECW*, 3:291

2   *Theory of Moral Sentiments* edited by D.D. Raphael and A.L. Macfie. Clarendon Press, Oxford, 1976, pp.85-86.

3   *An Inquiry into the Nature and Causes of the Wealth of Nations*, edited by R. H. Campbell and A. S. Skinner, Clarendon Press, Oxford, 1976, vol. 1, p.25.

4   Ibid. pp.36-7.

5   Ibid. p.343.

6   Ibid. p.75. It is worth noting that the meaning of the word 'natural' in this theoretical proposition is entirely different from that in Smith's social philosophy, where he talks of man's 'natural propensity' to better his condition.

7   Ibid. p.456. It is interesting that Smith makes the claim regarding the working of the invisible hand in book IV, chapter II 'Of Restraint upon the Importation from foreign Countries of such Goods as can be produced at Home' and not in book I, chapter VII where he discusses the theoretical proposition regarding the natural balance of the economy. He writes in book IV, chapter II: 'By preferring the support of domestick to that of foreign industry, he [the individual] intends only his own security; and by directing that industry in such a manner as its produce may be of the greatest value, he intends only his own gain, and he is in this, as in many other cases, led by an invisible hand to promote an end which was no part of his intention.' He makes the same point on p.454 in the same chapter and in book IV, chapter VII 'Of Colonies', p.630.

8   *MECW*, 3:290-91. Engel's reference to Adam Smith as 'the economic Luther' is made in his 'Outlines of a Critique of Political Economy' published in the *Deutsch-Französische Jahrbücher*. Ibid. p.422. It is interesting to note that Hegel had adopted a similar standpoint on the 'element of externality' in Catholic teaching. He wrote: 'The Lutheran doctrine therefore involves the entire substance of Catholicism, with the exception of all that results from the element of externality. Luther therefore could not do otherwise than refuse to yield an iota in regard to that doctrine of Eucharist in which the whole question is concentrated.' G.W.F. Hegel, *The Philosophy of History*, Dover Publications, New York, 1956, p.415.

9   *MECW*, 5:39. Incidentally, we find here the core idea of Marx's theory of historical development.

10 It is interesting that although at this point Marx has broken away from all 'previous materialism', including Feuerbach's, he still at this time (when he is writing *The Manuscripts*) regards Feuerbach's philosophy as being capable of providing a basis of communism. See Marx's letter of 11 August, 1844. *MECW*, 3:354.

11 *MECW*, 5:50. Marx's theory of development is discussed in chapter six.

12 *The Wealth of Nations*, vol. 1, p.360.

13 Ibid. p.22.
14 Ibid. pp.65-66.
15 Ibid. p.83.
16 Ibid. pp.83-84.
17 Ibid. p.86.
18 *MECW*, 3:278.
19 Ibid. p.247.
20 Ibid. p.272.
21 Ibid. p.275.
22 Ibid. p.274.
23 Giving credit to Hegel for having recognised this, Marx writes: 'Hegel's standpoint is that of political economy. He grasps *labour as the essence* of man ... [but] the only labour which Hegel knows and recognises *is abstractly mental labour.'* Ibid. p.333.
24 Ibid. p.277. see also p.278.
25 Ibid. p.278.
26 Marx uses the word 'wages' instead of the wage-system, but from the context it is clear that he means the latter.
27 Ibid. p.280.
28 *The Wealth of Nations*, vol. 1, p.85.
29 *MECW*, 3:284.
30 *MECW*, 3:245.
31 *MECW*, 3:252.
32 Ibid. p.251.
33 *MECW*, 4:150.
34 *MECW*, 4:36.
35 Ibid. p.37.

5

Brussels and Revolutions

Introduction

Marx arrived in Brussels in February 1845. (He had been deported from France.) His wife, with their daughter Jenny, joined him ten days later. A year later he renounced his Prussian citizenship as the Prussian government continued to demand his extradition. (By birth Marx was a Rhineland Prussian.) Three years later, in March 1848, he will be expelled from Belgium.

By the spring all the elements of Marx's worldview had been formulated. What was needed now was to connect them and present them in an integrated form. This point was made by Engels in his preface to the English edition of *The Communist Manifesto*. He wrote that when (in the spring of 1845) he arrived in Brussels, Marx had fully worked out his materialist conception and put before him in terms almost as clear as in which he had stated it in the preface. Engels made a similar statement in his 'On the History of the Communist League'.

The first work Marx composed after his arrival in Brussels consisted of his *Theses on Feuerbach*. These are 11 propositions or statements expressed in aphoristic form. These are the philosophical principles which constitute the basis of the new worldview. To quote Engels again, these propositions were invaluable as the first document in which was deposited 'the brilliant germ' of the new world outlook'.[1] The theses were not meant for publication. They were discovered in Marx's notebooks for 1844-47. The heading of these propositions was simply 'ad Feuerbach'. The title *Theses on Feuerbach* was given by Engels who first published them in an edited version in 1888. They were first published in their original form in 1924. (The main principles underlying the theses will be discussed in the next chapter.)

The next work Marx undertook (in collaboration with Engels) was *The German Ideology*. The first chapter of this two-volume book is a critique of Feuerbach's 'unhistorical' materialism. It is in this chapter that for the first (and the only) time an integrated account of the materialist conception is presented by Marx. The rest of the first volume is a long polemic against Bruno Bauer and Max Stirner, a German philosopher of anarchism, both opponents of socialism. Bauer is censured for his idealist views and contempt for ordinary people, and Stirner for his anarchism. The second volume is entirely devoted to a critique of 'true socialism', a tendency among certain German intellectuals who adopted a conciliatory attitude towards religion, advocated a 'petty bourgeois' form of utopian socialism, and opposed class struggle.[2]

The authors were unable to find a publisher for the book. Given the fact that by far the largest part of the book was devoted to polemics that were too long this is not surprising. The reason given by Marx and Engels for giving so much attention to a critique of Bauer and Stirner was that during this period they represented the 'ultimate consequences' of 'abstract' German philosophy and therefore the only philosophical opposition to communism. The attack on 'true socialism' was part of a wider ideological struggle waged by Marx and Engels against all existing socialist ideas that they considered petty bourgeois, sentimental or utopian. This first and elaborate exposition of the materialist conception of history was first published in 1932.

Within a year Marx produced another work, *The Poverty of Philosophy*. This book was a polemic against Proudhon, a critique of the latter's book, *Philosophy of Poverty*. It was completed in the first half of 1847 and published in Brussels and Paris simultaneously.

In this book Marx continued his discussion of the materialist conception as treated in *The German Ideology* and his polemic against 'bourgeois' socialist ideas. Here, Marx also touched upon certain fundamental problems of political economy. Marx later said that this book 'contains in embryo what after a labour of twenty years became the theory that was developed in *Capital*'.[3] This book contained the first published statement (brief and incomplete) of the new conception.

The last major work to be composed by Marx (with Engels) in Brussels was *The Communist Manifesto*. It was written in the months of December 1847 and January 1848. *The Manifesto* represented the culmination of the evolution of the Marxian vision. From this point on one could speak of a Marxian system of thought, an ideology of the working class, the driver of the revolutionary change this theory envisaged.

Also, from this time on the words 'communist' and 'communism' become uniquely associated with his name, thus distinguishing his idea of socialism from all other versions of it. His later scientific work – his 'critique of political economy' – will be set within the frame of this vision, and aimed specifically at giving theoretical effect to it.

Practical Political Activities

We observe that during Marx's stay in Brussels his theoretical endeavours and ideological struggle against all forms of utopian socialism and the philosophical notions of Young Hegelians are completely entwined with practical political activity. It was their duty, wrote Engels in 'On the History of the Communist League' to provide a scientific foundation for their view, but it was equally important for them to win over the European and in particular the German proletariat to their ideas.

During this period Marx also gave a series of lectures to the German Workers Society in Brussels on the subject of 'wages'. They were later published under the title *Wage Labour and Capital*.

When Marx arrived in Brussels he found there a large number of German exiles, mainly artisans, who held communist or socialist views. Many of them had fled from Paris after the failure of workers' uprisings there, in which they had participated, during the 1830s. Marx set about organising the Brussels communists into a coherent society based on his new world outlook. He also established a Brussels 'Communist Correspondence Committee' with the avowed aim of establishing fraternal contacts with communist groups in other European cities.

Engels was in Paris trying to set up a similar correspondence committee there, but without great success. The German expatriates there were under the influence of Karl Grün, a leading figure in German 'true socialism'. Grün was under the influence of Proudhon and later translated his *Philosophy of Poverty* into German.

At this time (before his attack on *The Philosophy of Poverty*), Marx wrote to Proudhon asking him if he would help with the setting up of a correspondence committee in Paris. In his letter Marx explained that the aim of the corresponding committees was to provide

> both a discussion of scientific questions and a critical appraisal of popular writings and socialist propaganda. But the main aim of our correspondence committees will be to put German socialists in touch with English and French socialists, to keep foreigners informed of the socialist movements that will develop in Germany and to inform the Germans in Germany of the progress of socialism in France and England.[4]

Proudhon (who had had a number of meetings with Marx during the latter's stay in Paris and knew something of his revolutionary ideas) declined the invitation. He lectured Marx in the following terms: 'I prefer to burn property in a slow fire rather than give it a new force in a St. Bartholomew's Night of property owners.' And added:

We should not give mankind new work by creating new confusion. Let us rather give the world an example of wise and far-seeing tolerance. We should not play the role of apostles of a new religion even if that religion is the religion of logic and reason.[5]

Marx also wrote to Louis Blanc, the French socialist leader, and Dr Ewerbeck, leader of the League of the Just in Paris, to set up a communist correspondence committee in Paris, but neither showed any enthusiasm for the proposal.

In his approach to Proudhon, Marx had been less than candid. He saw in various European cities assorted groups that all called themselves socialist or communist, but had different, and generally, confused views on socialism and on the means to achieve it. There were 'petty bourgeois' socialists, utopians, those who entertained romantic-feudal, Christian ideas of socialism, and others preaching justice and the brotherhood of man. For Marx, the communist correspondence committees were more than information bureaux. Their real task was to make them vehicles to combat utopian ideas and to bring these assorted groups into a single movement based on Marx's own brand of communism. It was, in fact, Marx's first attempt to set up some kind of an 'international', an umbrella under which various groups, all adhering to the new Marxist worldview, will coordinate their activities and support each other. His and Engels' aim was to teach the workers that their task was not the fulfilment of some utopian system but the conscious participation in the historical process of social revolution that they thought was taking place before their eyes.

To achieve these ends Marx, Engels and their communist friends used the columns of a German language twice-weekly newspaper that had been established in Brussels. The *Deutsche Brusseler Zeitung* had been launched by the former editor of the Paris journal *Vorwärts!* who had been deported from France along with Marx. To start with, the newspaper adopted a liberal-democratic line, but gradually it came increasingly under the influence of Marx and his friends so that it practically became the organ of Marxian communism.

Marx's articles in this newspaper were aimed at preparing the workers for their role in the bourgeois revolutions he thought were imminent in parts of Europe and to spread the new world outlook which was now giving the workers a tenable theoretical foundation for their struggle. (From this time on Marx starts to consistently use the word 'communism' to clearly distinguish his 'scientific' socialism from the utopian versions.)

In particular, one of Marx's main concerns at this time was to give communist groups in Germany a clear orientation with respect to the impending revolution in Germany. There was widespread reluctance in German communist groups to support the liberal bourgeoisie against the absolutist monarchy in Prussia. They saw the bourgeoisie as the direct oppressor of the working class. Marx was trying to convince them that the establishment of a liberal bourgeois democracy was a necessary stage in the progress of socialism and consequently communists should actively support the radical wing of the bourgeoisie. (On this issue his views had undergone change since his early Paris days. Then he had thought that a bourgeois revolution could be by-passed.) A letter written with Engels (on behalf of the Communist Correspondence Committee) advised a correspondent in Cologne:

> Join them (the bourgeoisie) for the time being in public demonstrations, proceed jesuistically, put aside your Teutonic probity, true-heartedness and decency, and push forward the bourgeois petitions for freedom of the press, a constitution, and so on. When this has been achieved a new era will dawn for C(ommunist) propaganda. Our means will be increased, the antithesis between bourgeoisie and proletariat will be sharpened.[6]

Marx was now clearly thinking in terms of a two-stage proletarian revolution, the bourgeois democratic revolution being an intermediate stage in the revolutionary struggle. He wrote: The proletarians 'can and must accept the bourgeois revolution as a pre-condition for the workers' revolution.'[7] In a long article with the title 'Moralising Criticism and Critical Morality', written in October 1847, Marx made the point that even if the proletariat overthrew bourgeois rule it would still have to complete the bourgeois revolution before it could go forward to a socialist revolution; this because of the material conditions prevailing at the time. Using here his newly-developed materialist conception, he wrote:

> Incidentally, if the bourgeoisie is politically, that is, by its state power, 'maintaining injustice in property relations', it is not creating it. The 'injustice in property relations' which is determined by the modern division of labour, the modern form of exchange, competition, concentration, etc., by no means arises from the political rule of the bourgeois class, but vice versa, the political rule of the bourgeois class arises from these modern relations of production ...If therefore the proletariat overthrows the political rule of the bourgeoisie, its victory will only be temporary, only an element in the bourgeois revolution itself, as in the year 1794, as long as in the course of history, in its 'movement', the material conditions have not yet been created which make necessary the abolition of the bourgeois mode of production and therefore also the definitive overthrow of the political rule of the bourgeoisie. The terror in France could thus by its mighty hammer-blows only serve to spirit away, as it were, the

ruins of feudalism from French soil. The timidly considerate bourgeoisie would not have accomplished this task in decades. The bloody action of the people thus only prepared the way for it. In the same way, the overthrow of the absolute monarchy would be merely temporary if the economic conditions for the rule of the bourgeois class had not yet become ripe. Men build a new world for themselves, not from the 'treasures of this earth', as grobian superstition imagines, but from the historical achievements of their declining world. In the course of their development they first have to produce the material conditions of a new society itself, and no exertion of mind can free them from this fate.[8]

The Communist League and *The Manifesto*

Marx's greatest success in organising correspondence committees was with the London League of the Just, which of all the communist groups in Europe was the best organised. Associated with it was a German Workers Educational Union which had about one thousand members, including some English and French. Unlike the League which was a secret organisation, the Union was an open association, its activities included lectures on political issues, lessons in English, and singing and dancing. The League had set up a correspondence committee and was in regular contact with Marx and Engels and had regularly received all the propaganda material produced by the Brussels Committee.

On 20 January 1847, the London Correspondence Committee sent one of their leaders, Joseph Moll, a German watchmaker, to Brussels to invite Marx and Engels to join the League. Moll also informed them that the central committee of the League planned to call a congress of the League in London. The central committee had issued a statement emphasising the need for a clear statement of the aims and objectives of the organisation. (Marx had earlier, in the summer of the previous year, suggested the idea of a congress in London to develop a theoretical basis for the activities of the League.)

The congress was held in London in the summer of 1847 (2-9 June). Engels represented Paris, but Marx was unable to attend. Instead, he sent a friend of his, Wilhelm Wolff, to represent Brussels. The congress changed the name of the League of the Just to Communist League and agreed in general terms that the aim of the communists was to overthrow the rule of the bourgeoisie and abolish private property. The statutes of the League were amended to give it a more democratic structure and to change its slogan from 'all men are brothers' to 'proletarians of all countries unite!' (Marx had earlier said there were many men whose brother he would prefer not to be.) It was decided to convene a second congress to take its programme further. Later in the year (August) Marx converted the Brussels Communist Correspondence Committee into a branch of the Communist League. He was elected its president.

The second congress was held on 29 November (1847). Discussions lasted ten days. The statutes of the League were further amended to remove all remaining elements of a utopian nature. Marx's worldview had completely prevailed. Engels later wrote: 'All contradictions and doubt were finally set at rest, [and] the new principles were unanimously adopted.'[9]

Marx and Engels were charged with the responsibility of drafting the League's manifesto on the lines of their standpoint, and submit it to the central committee by the middle of December. The manifesto, enunciating the fundamental principles of communism, was drafted by Marx and Engels during the months of December 1847 and January 1848. *The Manifesto of the Communist Party* was published by the League (which by now had ceased to be a secret society) in London in February.

Revolutions in Europe

Hardly had the proverbial ink dried on *The Manifesto* than the news of the revolution in Paris reached Brussels. The 'bourgeois king' Louis Philippe was overthrown, France was declared a republic and a new provisional French government set up. There were repercussions in Brussels. German expatriate communists who had enjoyed relative freedom came under suspicion. Marx, along with a number of his comrades and his wife, was arrested. On 3 March he and his friends received orders to leave Belgium within 24 hours. The same day he received an invitation from the provisional government in Paris welcoming him to France. The following day Marx, his wife and three children (two were born during their stay in Brussels) were taken to the border and deported. A day later they arrived in Paris.

Soon after Marx's arrival in Paris, there was a revolutionary uprising in Vienna (March 13, 1848). The emperor accepted all the demands of the insurrectionists. There was a similar uprising in Berlin (March 18 and 19) and the king was forced to make concessions, installed a new government led by a well know liberal democratic businessman, Ludolf Camphausen, and proclaimed freedom of the press and association. There were also uprisings in other German cities. A new Prussian national assembly was to be elected on the basis of adult franchise and an indirect voting system. It was to be charged with the task of framing a new constitution 'by agreement with the Crown.'

Marx, with Engels, concentrated his efforts on the large number of German expatriates in Paris. The leaders of the Communist League founded a German Workers Club to explain to German migrants in Paris the task facing them in the bourgeois democratic revolution. An important task of the Club members, which numbered around 300, was to struggle against a large number of German expatriates, including some League members, who were organising a 'German Legion' and collecting arms to support the revolutionary movements in various German cities. Marx and Engels believed such plans to be 'adventurist', seeking to export revolution into Germany. Engels wrote later:

> We opposed this [the German Legion's] playing with revolution in the most decisive fashion. To carry out an invasion, which was to import the revolution forcibly from outside, into the midst of the ferment then going on in Germany, meant to undermine the revolution in Germany itself, to strengthen the governments and to deliver the legionaries ... defenceless in the hands of the German troops.[10]

The legionaries did carry out the 'invasion' and were annihilated by government troops.

Marx and the other League leaders took the view that with around 300 club members it was not practical to form an independent force. Club members should instead return to Germany individually or in small groups and spread themselves around the cities and reinforce revolutionary events that were taking place. And taking advantage of the right to free association establish workers' associations in different towns and cities, hoping later to create a national network.

By this time Marx had received from the central committee of the Communist League executive authority to form a new central leadership. The new committee (referred to as the Central Authority) formed by Marx included himself, Engels, Wilhelm Wolff, and the three leaders of the League from London, Heinrich Bauer, Joseph Moll and Karl Schapper.

The committee formulated 17 demands ('in the interest of the proletariat, the petty bourgeoisie and the peasantry') that constituted the political programme in the current situation. These were incorporated in a document with the title 'The Demands of the Communist Party in Germany'. A large number of copies were printed as leaflets for distribution among German expatriates who were now returning to Germany. 'The Demands of the Communist Party in Germany' were also printed in a number of newspapers in Germany.

The 'Demands' were based on Marx's view (already indicated) that what was now taking place in Germany was a bourgeois democratic revolution which was a necessary pre-condition for a proletarian revolution. It was therefore the duty of the communists to support the radical wing of the bourgeoisie in order to achieve a liberal democratic political order that would do away with the vestiges of feudalism and prepare the ground for a proletarian revolution. The 'Demands' included unification of Germany (which at the time was fragmented into more than 30 states and statelets); elections to the legislative assembly on the basis of adult franchise; abolition of all obligations imposed on peasants; nationalisation of feudal estates, mines and means of transport; the establishment of a state bank; complete separation of the state and the church; universal and free education for all; and universal arming of the people to defend the revolution. The document opened with the Communist League slogan 'Workers of all countries, unite!', and concluded with the words:

> It is in the interest of the German proletariat, the petty bourgeoisie and the small peasants to support these demands with all possible energy. Only by the realisation of these demands will the millions in Germany, who have been exploited by a handful of persons and whom the exploiters would like to keep in further subjection, win the rights and attain to that power to which they are entitled as the producers of all wealth.[11]

Using his executive authority, Marx suspended the Communist League. He took the view that to join the revolution under the banner of an organisation that had the reputation of a secret society was not the correct policy in the prevailing situation in which propaganda could be conducted openly.

The Marx family and Engels left Paris for Germany in the first week of April.

Marx established himself in Cologne, a large city located in the heart of Germany's most industrialised and politically advanced region, a city he knew well and where he had many contacts. Four years earlier he had edited the newspaper *Rheinische Zeitung* there with great verve and success. On his arrival there he applied to the Cologne city council for citizenship which, as noted, he had renounced from Brussels. The application was accepted by the Council. It was subject to approval by the government in Berlin which rejected it.

There was already, before the arrival of Marx and his friends, a Cologne Workers' Association which included workers, artisans, unemployed workers and small shopkeepers. The Association now became a centre of revolutionary agitation among the workers. Three months later a more broad-based organisation than the Association, the Rhenish District Committee of Democrats was founded. Marx together with Schapper and Moll became its member. A lawyer, Karl Schneider, was elected president.

Marx's own revolutionary activity was largely confined to journalism and work with the Committee of Democrats. He made frantic efforts to raise funds to launch a newspaper. On the strength of his reputation as a competent editor of the *Rheinische Zeitung* during 1842-3, he was able to raise some money from liberal businessmen and professionals. But that was not enough. He put into the project part of his own money which he had recently received from his mother as an advance on his inheritance. Engels, who was living on an allowance from his father, made a small contribution. The first issue of the *Neue Rheinische Zeitung* appeared on the first of June. There was an editorial board, including Engels, but Marx had complete control over policy.

The general policy of the newspaper followed the lines of the 'Demands of the Communist Party in Germany', and it was indicated by the slogan on its masthead – 'Organ of Democracy'. The policy clearly stated that during the course of the revolution the struggle of the workers against their capitalist employers was to be suspended. At the same time the newspaper would attack the weaknesses and vacillations of the bourgeois liberals who had formed government in Berlin. As we will see the tone of the newspaper changed radically during the course of the revolution.

The newspaper was hugely successful; it became one of the largest circulation newspapers in Germany.

By the end of the summer, it was clear that the revolutionary forces, largely local and fragmented and lacking any central direction, were losing momentum. While the opposition was diverse and divided the autocratic structure of the Prussian state – the army and the bureaucracy – remained intact. The bourgeoisie was unwilling to go all the way to complete the revolution.

In early November, the King of Prussia dismissed the liberal government and installed a general as prime minister. Later he forcibly moved the seat of the Prussian Assembly away from Berlin to a small provincial town. The Assembly protested but without achieving any significant results. In Vienna the royalist forces successfully counter-attacked and restored the emperor, who had fled the city, to the throne. Marx knew that this was the beginning of the end of the bourgeois revolution.

In an article, 'The bourgeoisie and the counter-revolution in Vienna', published on 7 November, Marx stated his new, more militant position. He blamed the success of the counter-revolution in Vienna on 'the treachery' of the right-wing of the bourgeoisie. He wrote:

> The purposeless massacres perpetrated since the June and October events, the tedious offering of sacrifices since February and March, the very cannibalism of the counter-revolution will convince the nation that there is only one means by which the murderous death agonies of the old society and the bloody birth throes of the new society can be shortened, simplified and concentrated – and that is by revolutionary terrorism.[12]

In early December the Prussian king administered his final coup. He dismissed the Prussian Assembly and declared that he himself would issue a new constitution. For this Marx blamed the liberal bourgeoisie which he thought had failed to take decisive action. Already, before the dissolution of the Assembly, Marx had, in an article entitled 'Counter-Revolution in Berlin', stated that the bourgeoisie

> would have liked so much to transform the feudal monarchy into a bourgeois monarchy in an amicable way... the bourgeois party would have liked to unite with the feudal party and together with it to enslave the people. But the old bureaucracy does not want to be reduced to the status of a servant of a bourgeoisie for whom, until now, it had been a despotic tutor.[13]

In the same article Marx called on the 'Rhine Province to hasten to the assistance of the Berlin Assembly with men and weapons.' He also urged the people not to pay taxes. 'No taxes are to be paid to the government guilty of treason', proclaimed the *Neue Rheinische Zeitung* on its front page.[14] The committee of the Rhineland Democrats met under the chairmanship of Marx and issued a call to the people urging them to refuse to pay taxes, organise a levy for defence against the 'enemy', and to create 'committees of public safety' (presumably, on lines of the committees formed during the 'reign of terror' in revolutionary France in 1793-94).

During the period of the counter-revolution, Marx wrote a number of articles specifically on the nature of the revolution. Three points are worth making.

First, Marx argued that the success of a revolution required a revolutionary dictatorship that would strike at the old state structure. This, the liberal bourgeoisie, when it was given power by the king (March 1848), was unwilling or unable to do. It wanted to work on a 'legal basis'. This failure was at least in part responsible for the King's successful coup. In an article 'Crisis and the Counter-Revolution', Marx wrote:

> Every provisional political set-up following a revolution requires a dictatorship, and an energetic dictatorship at that. From the very beginning we blamed Camphausen for not having acted in a dictatorial manner, for not having immediately smashed up and removed the remains of the old institutions. While thus Camphausen indulged in constitutional day dreaming, the defeated party strengthened its position within the bureaucracy and in the army and occasionally even risked open fight.[15]

Second, in an article 'The Bourgeoisie and the Counter-Revolution', Marx drew a sharp distinction between the contemporary bourgeois revolution and the English and French bourgeois revolutions. The latter type of revolution took place at a time when the working people had not come to form an independent class, they and the non-bourgeois strata of the middle class had not yet any interest separate from the bourgeoisie.

Therefore, when they opposed the bourgeoisie, as they did in

1793 and 1794, they fought only for the attainment of the aims of the bourgeoisie, even if not in the manner of the bourgeoisie. All French terrorism was nothing but plebeian way of dealing with the enemies of the bourgeoisie, absolutism, feudalism and philistinism.[16]

By contrast, in 1848, when the German bourgeoisie confronted feudalism and absolutism it was at the time menacingly confronted by the proletariat and other sections of society whose interests were related to those of the proletariat. Marx wrote:

> Unlike the bourgeoisie of 1789, the Prussian bourgeoisie, when it confronted the monarchy and aristocracy, the representatives of the old society, was not speaking for the whole of the modern society. It had sunk to the level of a kind of social estate as clearly distinct from the crown as it was from the people, with a strong bent to oppose both adversaries and irresolute towards each of them individually because it always saw both of them either in front of it or behind it.[17]

The conclusion Marx arrived at was that in the existing conditions a 'purely' bourgeois revolution will have to be realised under the leadership of the working class; it will be the first stage in a 'permanent revolution' which would destroy the remnants of feudalism and absolutism, leading eventually to proletarian revolution.

Third, Marx came to the conclusion that any revolution confined to a single country could not succeed; to succeed it had to be part of an international movement that would confront the Europe-wide counter-revolutionary bloc. He believed that the defeat of the Paris proletariat in June (1848) had given a signal for a general counter-revolutionary onslaught across Europe. (After the February revolution when the king was overthrown and the country declared a republic, there was, in June, a workers' uprising which was brutally suppressed.) Marx thought that the Prussian king's coup was a direct result of the suppression of the Paris uprising and of the revolutionary forces in Vienna in late October and early November.

In a short article 'The Revolutionary Movement', published on 1 January (1849), Marx wrote:

> The defeat of the working class in June was at the same time the renewed fettering of the nationalities who had responded to the crowing of the Gallic cock [the February revolution] with heroic attempts to liberate themselves. Prussian, Austrian and English *sbirri* [policemen] once more plundered, ravished and murdered in Poland, Italy and Ireland.

Another, uprising in Paris, this time successful, he thought, could lead to the liberation of Europe.[18]

However, he immediately introduced a highly practical consideration. Every attempt to carry out a revolution to a successful conclusion in France will be thwarted by military intervention by England, the most powerful country in Europe.

A revolution in England was therefore a precondition for a Europe-wide revolution. Thus only when the Chartists could successfully carry out a social revolution will such a revolution pass from the realm of utopia to reality. A revolution in France will lead to a European war:

> England will head the counter-revolutionary armies just as it did during the Napoleonic period, but through the war itself it will be thrown to the head of the revolutionary movement and it will repay the debt it owes in regard to the revolution of the 18th century.[19]

With the progress of the counter-revolution (in the spring and summer of 1849) it was clear that the days of *Neue Rheinische Zeitung* were numbered. First, Marx, along with Engels and the publisher of the newspaper, Hermann Korff, was charged with libel against state officials. Marx used the occasion to lecture the jury on the causes of the failure of the revolution. The sympathetic jury acquitted all three.

Marx was accused (for the second time), along with Schapper and Schneider of the Committee of Democrats, for having issued the no-tax proclamation, and for plotting to overthrow the government. Marx again lectured the jury on his views on the nature of the revolution. The defendants were acquitted. The jury foreman thanked Marx for an informative lecture.

By now the *Neue Rheinische Zeitung* was in dire financial difficulties. Marx had thrown all the money he and his wife had in support of the paper. In the second half of April (1849), Marx had toured parts of North-Western Germany and Westphalia to raise funds, and also to make contacts with various workers' organisations and members of the Communist League to discuss the future of communist activities in the country. Marx was unable to secure financial support.

On his return to Cologne, Marx learnt that he was to be expelled from the country. A week later (16 May) he received orders to leave Prussian territories within 24 hours.

In the last issue of the newspaper (19 May) Marx repeated (in an article with the title 'The Summary Suppression of the *Neue Rheinische Zeitung*') what he had said in his article 'Victory of the counter-revolution in Vienna': revolutionary terror was the only means by which the death throes of the old society and the birth of the new could be shortened.

Addressing the Prussian authorities, Marx warned: 'We have no compassion and we ask no compassion from you. When our turn comes, we shall not make excuses for the terror.'[20]

In a short article addressed 'To the the Workers of Cologne' he warned that in the current situation when the counter-revolution had triumphed they should not undertake any insurrection 'as a state of siege in Cologne would demoralise the entire Rhine Province, and a state of siege would be the inevitable consequence of any rising on your part at this moment.' The address concluded with the declaration that the editors' last word 'everywhere and always will be: the emancipation of the working class.'[21]

The Marx family and Engels left Cologne on 19 May and went to Bingen, in Hesse. From there Marx and Engels travelled to Frankfurt to appeal to the Left members of the National Assembly to support the revolutionary movement that was still alive in South-West Germany. Unsuccessful there, they went to Baden hoping to persuade the leaders of the insurrection there to march on Frankfurt, again without success. Marx returned to Bingen, Engels joined the movement in Baden. On the 2 June, Marx left for Paris, while his wife Jenny with her three children went to Trier to be with her mother.

Marx was still expecting a revolutionary upheaval in France. In fact, the revolutionary game in Europe was up. The last insurrections in Germany were petering out; the Hungarian nationalist revolution was crushed by Russian troops; in Italy, the French were re-establishing papal authority. There were peaceful demonstrations in Paris, but they were easily suppressed. The 'party of order' was now in full control.

On 19 July, Marx and his family (who had by now joined him) received orders expelling them from Paris. He was given permission to live in the department of Morbihan in Brittany, but refused the offer. On 24 August (1849) Marx sailed for England. His wife and children were to follow him later. Now 31, he had little idea that he would be spending the rest of the 34 years of his life in England.

NOTES

1 *MESW*, 2:359. .
2 The book as it stands now was put together from various manuscripts by the first editors of the Marx-Engels collected works. See *MECW*, 5:586-88.
3 *MECW*, 6:xviii.
4 Quoted in McLellan, *Karl Marx – His Life and Thought*, p.154
5 Mehring, *Karl Marx – The Story of his Life*, pp.119-20.
6 *MECW*, 6:56
7 Ibid. p.333.
8 Ibid. p. 319-20.
9 'On the History of the Communist League', *MESW*, 2:348.
10 Ibid. pp.351-52.
11 *MECW*, 7: 3-7.
12 Ibid. pp.505-06.
13 *MECW*, 8:15-16.
14 Ibid. p.19.
15 *MECW*, 7:431.
16 *MECW*, 8:161.
17 Ibid. p.162.
18 Ibid. p.214.
19 Ibid. p.215.
20 *MECW*, 9:453.
21 Ibid. p.467.

6

The Materialist Conception of History I:
The Conceptual Framework

Theses on Feuerbach – A New Version of Materialism

As noted in the preceding chapter, the first work Marx composed after coming to Brussels consisted of 11 propositions, referred to as the *Theses on Feuerbach*. They were formulated as a critique of Feuerbach's philosophical standpoint from which he now completely emancipated his own thinking. Marx now had his own philosophical standpoint or method to underpin his vision of the social process. He refers to his own version of materialism as 'practical', 'communist' materialism. He writes in *The German Ideology*, for 'the practical materialist, i.e., the communist, it is a question of revolutionising the existing world, of practically coming to grips with and changing things found in existence.'[1]

It is in the first *Thesis* that Marx suggests his own version. In it Marx rejects all 'old' materialism, including Feuerbach's. According to the *Thesis* it led to passivity; it conceived sensuous reality only in the form of object, not as sensuous human activity; it did not conceptualise observed reality subjectively, not as practice. The *Thesis* observes that it was idealism that, in contradiction to old materialism, emphasised the active side. But of course it could do that only 'abstractly', for idealism does not know 'real sensuous activity as such'. The main criticism directed at Feuerbach's materialism is that it led him to regard the theoretical attitude as the only genuine human activity, thus treating practice with disdain. Marx will incorporate the active element of idealism into his materialism.

This clearly needs explaining. For instance, what does Marx mean when he says that reality should be conceived 'subjectively', as 'sensuous human activity?

Let us start by defining the old materialism that Marx is rejecting. This idea was recently expressed by a scientist in the following terms:

> The history of science is partly the history of an idea that is by now so familiar that it no longer astounds; the universe, including our own existence, can be explained by the little bits of matter. We do so, to some extent at least, by a kind of reduction. The stuff of biology, for instance, can be reduced to chemistry and the stuff of chemistry can be reduced to physics.[3]

In this version of materialism reality is taken as given, as objective datum, it is 'out there'; according to it our knowledge of the world, ideas, indeed our ideals, plans for the future are all determined by some kind of mechanical impulses. One implication of this version is that in order to understand historical development we would have to assume some kind of a dynamic urge in matter. Marx saw that this way of thinking led to passivism, acceptance of reality as it is. And that is what he was rejecting.

In contrast with this approach, Marx's version of materialism sees reality, things, not as given datum, but as 'sensuous human activity'. This means that the act of knowing, understanding reality involves our acting on, engaging with, the object, that reality is shaped by man, man's consciousness. This is what Marx means when he says that reality should be seen as 'sensuous human activity. Having rejected the old determinist version, Marx incorporates into his own version the insight provided by Hegel for whom reality, actuality is not external, not objective, but is shaped by spirit; the spirit moves, develops and reality is shaped and developed with it. This is the activist element that Marx took from Hegel. He substitutes active man for Hegel's active spirit.

The idea that reality is the product of man is explained in detail in *The* (a point already touched upon in Chapter 4.)[4] The 'sensuous world', the 'objects', reality that we observe are the result of historical social development, the result of the activity of a succession of generations.

Marx emphasises this point again and again because although Feuerbach was a materialist in the sense that he saw reality in 'sensuous' terms, he took reality as given and this led him to shun any political activity:

> ...we understand that the celebrated 'unity of man with nature' has always existed in industry and has existed in varying forms in every epoch according to less or greater development of industry, and so is the 'struggle' of man with nature right up to the development of his productive forces on a corresponding basis... so much is this activity, this unceasing sensuous labour and creation, this production, the foundation of the whole sensuous world as it now exists that, were it interrupted only

for a year, Feuerbach would find not only an enormous change in the natural world, but would very soon find that the whole world of men and his own perceptive faculty, nay his own existence, were missing. Of course, in all this the priority of external nature remains unassailed, and all this has no application to the original men produced by *generatio aequivoca* [spontaneous generation]; but this differentiation has meaning only insofar as man is considered to be distinct from nature. For that matter, nature, the nature that preceded human history, is not by any means the nature in which Feuerbach lives, it is nature which today no longer exists anywhere (except perhaps on a few Australian coral islands of recent origin) and which, therefore does not exist for Feuerbach either.[5]

We have here core idea underlying Marx's approach to understanding historical development. The 'original' man confronted nature – nature as it existed before man appeared on the scene – acted upon it, altered it. The reality we observe today is the result of the activity of generations and generations of men, coming one after the other, each changing and modifying the inheritance received from the preceding generation. This is the reality that Marx refers to as 'sensuous human activity', unity of man and nature, historical nature. Reality is not a given datum for man as such, though for any particular generation the inheritance from the past is given, on which it acts, modifies it and passes it on to the next generation.

Marx had rejected Hegel's idealism early in his intellectual development and adopted the view that ideas or forms of consciousness have no independent existence. He wrote:

> They have no history, no development; but men, developing their material production and their material intercourse, alter, along with this their actual world, also their thinking and the products of their thinking. It is not consciousness that determines life, but life that determines consciousness. For the first manner of approach [idealism] the starting-point is consciousness taken as the living individual; while for the second manner of approach [Marx's own], which conforms to life, it is the real living individuals themselves, and consciousness is considered solely as their consciousness.[6]

While rejecting the idealist notion that ideas have independent existence and history, he at the same time gave human beings, their minds, their consciousness an active, creative role. Ideas arise in the brains of human beings engaged in productive activity. But human consciousness cannot create anything out of nothing. Humanity must have something material to work on, as, for instance, 'the nature that preceded human history' for the 'original men' or, as the inheritance received by any generation from the receding generation. This is the extent of Marx's materialism.

Not a 'General Historical-Philosophical Theory', But a Conceptual Framework

In the following section we present the leading ideas of the materialist conception. Does this conception or model or worldview seek to describe reality, give a picture, though a simplified one, of reality, or is it a method of understanding reality? This question is discussed in this section.

We start with the fact that Marx never published a complete statement of his materialist conception. As noted, *The German Ideology*, the only work where the new conception was systematically presented, remained unpublished in Marx's life time. There is no evidence that after its first rejection by a publisher Marx made any further attempt to have it published. In 1859 he wrote:

> We abandoned the manuscript to the gnawing criticism of the mice all the more willingly as we had achieved our main purpose – self-clarification.[7]

In December 1846, Marx gave a fairly integrated statement of the main aspects of the new conception in an 11-page letter to P. V. Annenkov, a Russian man of letters, but obviously this letter was not meant for publication. Annenkov, who had met Marx in Brussels, had asked for his views on *The Philosophy of Poverty*, a book Proudhon had recently published. Annenkov of course knew nothing of the development of the materialist conception, but Marx, who had just completed (with Engels) *The German Ideology*, perhaps took this opportunity to clarify further his thoughts on the subject.[8]

The first published reference to the conception appeared in Marx's *The Poverty of Philosophy*, a polemic against Proudhon. In this work (as Marx put it in the 1859 preface) only 'the decisive points' of the conception were 'indicated', and these remarks arose incidentally when Marx was criticising Proudhon's use of the Hegelian philosophy in the exposition of his own economic theory or, in Marx's words, when Proudhon wanted 'to frighten the French by flinging quasi-Hegelian phrases at them'.[9]

In *The Communist Manifesto* the new conception is applied, it does not contain a systemic exposition.

The first direct, though brief (only a page and half), statement of the materialist conception appeared in print 13 years later, in the much quoted 1859 preface. It appeared when Marx was tracing his own intellectual development, and, interestingly, it is incomplete in that it does not make any direct reference to the centrality of class struggle in the materialist conception. Marx here referred to the conception as 'a general result [rather than a theory] at which I arrived and which, once won, served as a guiding thread for my studies...'[10]

In the 'afterword' [postface] to the second edition of *Capital*, written in 1873, Marx referred to the materialist conception as 'materialist basis of my method'.[11]

Marx had a similar thinking about his theory of capitalism (based on the application of the materialist method). In a letter written in 1877 to a Russian journal he denied that his 'historical sketch' of the genesis of capitalism in Western Europe was a general theory. Referring to a critic of his *Capital*, Marx wrote:

> He [the critic] absolutely insists on transforming my historical sketch of the genesis of capitalism in Western Europe into a historico-philosophical theory of the general course fatally imposed on all peoples, whatever the historical circumstances in which they find themselves placed, in order to arrive ultimately at the economic formation [communism] which ensures the greatest expansion of the productive forces of social labour, as well as the most complete development of man. But I beg his pardon.

And he added:

> [E]vents of striking similarity, taking place in different historical contexts, led to totally disparate results. By studying each of these developments separately, and comparing them, one may easily discover the key to this phenomenon [the question whether Russia could skip capitalism and go straight to socialism]. But success will never come with the master-key of a general historico-philosophical theory, whose supreme virtue consists in being supra-historical.[12]

In a letter of March 1881, written to a Russian correspondent, Marx referred to his theory of capitalism as 'my so-called theory' and quoted from the French edition of his *Capital* the following statement: 'The 'historical inevitability' of this course [capitalist development] therefore is expressly restricted to the countries of Western Europe.' This followed from the observation that other countries of Western Europe were observed to be following the English experience with regard to the 'complete separation of ... the producer from the means of production.'[13]

All this is to emphasise that the materialist conception was not intended by Marx to describe social reality; nor was it a model from which social reality could be deduced. It was a conceptual framework or a model used as a guide to interpreting reality – historical development and, in particular, the working of the capitalist mode of production. It was not claimed that historical development followed a definite pattern in which, through some internal necessity, one mode of production inevitably evolved within the womb of the preceding mode. Such a claim was made only in the case of capitalism that evolved within the frame of feudalism in Western Europe. Marx recognised that there were societies (the 'Asiatic mode of Production') that had shown no sign of internal development; that the European feudal society did not evolve in the 'womb' of the ancient society – there were a variety of factors for its emergence, including (as *The German Ideology* noted) 'the conquest by the barbarians', and the 'influence of the German military constitution.'[14]

And Marx never attempted to argue that the development of capitalism was driven by 'forces of production'.

Now, it is true that Marx did believe that socialism or communism would evolve within the working of capitalism, but this idea was not deduced from the model; it was based, using the materialist conception as a guide, on the study of observed tendencies ('laws of motion') in the working of contemporary capitalism. (Marx may have been wrong to give to various tendencies the weights that he did, but that is altogether a different matter.) Marx's communism was 'scientific' because this idea was derived from such observed tendencies, and it was thus distinguished from utopian socialism which was said to be unhistorical and based on fantasies.

To conclude: the fact that Marx never thought it necessary to broadcast his materialist conception in a systematic manner is important. He was not offering an overarching theory of history, but developed a model, a method for investigating and understanding the sources and direction of social change. In his own analysis of contemporary and historical events he used the model flexibly, often, as we will see, discussing events in a manner that did not fit the model.

The Materialist Conception – The 'Premises'

The first premise refers to the material conditions of production and the concept of reproduction. The exposition of the new standpoint starts with the premise, first, that in order to live (and make history) men must first produce their subsistence. That they do, in the first instance, in certain definite material conditions, 'mass of productive forces', methods of production, that consist of productive equipment, tools, and appropriate capacities and skills needed to use those equipment and tools, etc., that are actually in existence. Every generation starts with these inherited material conditions – inherited from the preceding generation. The generation in question uses the inherited means of production and subsistence, improves upon them and then passes them on to the next generation.

History is nothing but the succession of the separate generations, each of which uses the materials, capital funds, the productive forces handed down to it by the preceding generations, and thus, on the one hand, continues the traditional activities in completely changed circumstances, and on the other, modifies the old circumstances with a completely changed activity.[15]

It may be noted in passing that if each generation simply passed on to the next the material conditions, etc. – without any modification or improvement, it would be a case of 'simple' reproduction, there would then be no history. History is made because something new is added to the inheritance received,

It should be emphasised that productive forces are more than mere material objects. A locomotive in itself is not a productive force. A society that has inherited this technology also inherits the capacity not only to use it but also the knowledge to produce it and all the inputs that go into its production and the complementary products that make it operational.

The second premise refers to the complementarity between conditions of production and social structure and social relations.

To any given stage in the development of the economy there corresponds a form of social 'intercourse', a term used in *The German Ideology*, later replaced by 'social relations' or 'relations of production'. In the letter written to Annenkov (referred to earlier), Marx wrote:

> Assume a particular state of development in the productive faculties of men and you will get a corresponding form of production, commerce and consumption and you will have a corresponding form of social constitution, a corresponding organisation of family, of orders or of classes, in a word, a corresponding civil society.[16]

Marx expressed the same idea in his 1859 preface:

> In the social production of their life, men enter into definite relations that are indispensable and independent of their will, relations which correspond to a definite stage of development of their material productive forces. The sum total of these relations of production constitutes the economic structure of society ...[17]

In social production, a cooperative enterprise, people get into all kind of relations. Marx's focus is on relations that arise in production, between owners of the means of production and those who work for them. The social structure of society is seen in terms of these relations.

The third premise refers to the relationship between the sphere of material production and the social structure corresponding to it, which form the 'base', and the realm of consciousness, that is, ideas, general culture, belief systems, politics, etc., which form the 'superstructure'. The central idea in this premise is simple: mankind's powers of reasoning emerged and developed in grappling with the material conditions of life, in the process of making its daily living. It is in our daily work, in collaboration with others, in the prevailing relations of production that we develop our ways of thinking.

Marx wrote:

> The production of ideas, of conceptions, of consciousness, is at first directly interwoven with the material activity and the material intercourse of men – the language of real life. Conceiving, thinking, the mental intercourse of men at this stage still appears as the direct efflux of their material behaviour. The same applies to mental production as expressed in the language of the politics, laws, morality, religion, metaphysics, etc., of a people. Men are the real producers of their conceptions, ideas, etc., that is, real active men, as they are conditioned by a definite development of their productive forces and the intercourse corresponding to these, up to its furthest forms. Consciousness can never be anything else than conscious being, and the being of men is their actual life-process...

> In contrast to German philosophy which descends from heaven to earth, here it is a matter of ascending from earth to heaven... The phantoms formed in the brains of men are also, necessarily, sublimates of their material life-process, which is empirically verifiable and bound to material premises. Morality, religion and all the rest of ideology as well as the forms of consciousness corresponding to these, thus no longer retain the semblance of independence... It is not consciousness that determines life, but life that determines consciousness. For the first manner of approach [German idealist philosophy] the starting-point is consciousness taken as a living individual; for the second manner of approach [Marx's own], which conforms to real life, it is the real living individuals themselves, and consciousness is considered solely as their consciousness.[18]

There are two further related assumptions of this approach to the understanding of historical development. According to the first, the reality that we know from experience is an evolutionary process, and that this process is organic in character – an idea that follows from the way that Marx conceptualised society – organic as opposed to atomistic. The second assumption is that social change – the evolutionary process – is driven by some internal 'necessities', so that no extraneous factor is needed to move the system forward. This approach may be contrasted with that suggested by analogy with Newtonian mechanics according to which the system, the economy, will stay put unless moved by an external force. Without this assumption historical development would be simply the result of unpredictable extraneous factors, and there could then be no theory of development. It becomes the task of the new theory to identify the internal 'necessities' that drive the economy and society forward.

The source of internal change in the new theory lies in production, in the economy: people must produce in order to live and procreate, and reproduce their life. This, the need to produce, is the first premise of human existence and therefore of all human history. This is the first point. Marx writes:

> The second point is that the satisfaction of the first need, the action of satisfying and the instruments of satisfaction which have been acquired, leads to new needs; and this creation of new needs is the first historical act.[19]

We have here the central idea of the new conception. Every generation receives from the preceding generation a set of needs and the means of satisfying these needs. This inheritance prescribes the limits within which the generation in question works; in the course of satisfying these needs, new needs arise and new methods are developed to satisfy these needs. As Marx writes:

> ... each stage contains a material result, a sum of production forces, a historically created relation to nature and of individuals to one another, which is handed down to each generation from its predecessor; a mass of productive forces, capital funds and circumstances, which on the one hand is indeed modified by the new generation, but on the other also prescribes for it its conditions of life and gives it a definite development, a special character. It shows that circumstances make men just as men make circumstances.[20]

To conclude: social evolution or historical development has its roots in economic development. Changes in forms of social organisation, political developments, our ways of thinking, the way we practice religion, scientific progress, our culture in general are necessary adaptations to changes in the economy. To put it another way, an economy that is stagnating, in which the same needs are being met by the same methods of production generation after generation will not experience any significant change in terms of developments in politics, culture and scientific knowledge.

It should be noted that the account of the historical process as presented in the preceding paragraphs can be considered as ideologically neutral; that is to say, it can be accepted by those who do not subscribe to the ideal of a socialist or communist society.[21]

We turn now to those features that make the materialist conception (as Marx put it) 'communist', 'practical' (that is, uniquely Marxian) conception.

Theory of Social Classes and the Concept of Mode of Production

We consider societies where the development of productive forces has reached a point that people produce more than what is required to satisfy the basic needs of subsistence. In other words, society produces a surplus of goods over and above what constitutes its necessary consumption.

In such a society there is scope for the emergence of private property, and for one class of people to control means of production. We then have two classes of people, those who control means of production and those who must labour for them in order to live.

In this way Marx locates the existence of classes in the sphere of production. This was a new insight, a point that Marx noted in a letter written in 1852. He acknowledged that bourgeois historians had described the development of the struggle between classes and that they had studied the economic anatomy of the classes, but what he had shown (among other things) was that 'the existence of classes is only bound up with particular historical phases in the development of production.'[22]

The result of this approach is two-fold.

First, the relationship between the two classes is one of power of one over the other – a power that arises from the ownership of the means of production – and this power enables the dominant class to appropriate the surplus product. The relationship thus becomes essentially one of antagonism.

Second, these economic classes also become social classes, that is, society is seen fundamentally to be divided between these two classes, and this social relation becomes the focal point of the social structure. In other words, the social structure is understood in terms of these two economic classes.

It is appropriate at this point to introduce the related concept of the mode of production. A mode of production is a distinct form of economic and social organisation, the central features of which refer to the form in which property is held, the form that the relationship between the propertied and the labouring class takes, and the manner in which the surplus product is appropriated by the dominant class.

In *The German Ideology* reference is made to four distinct types of mode of production: the tribal society (extended family) headed by a patriarchal chieftain, slavery-based ancient Greece and Rome, feudalism of the Middle Ages, and the modern bourgeois society. In *The Communist Manifesto* only the last three are mentioned. In the slavery-based society the slave is the property of the slave-owner and the appropriation of the surplus product simply follows from that fact; under feudalism the main form of property is inalienable land held by a feudal lord, the peasant owns his means of production in the form of agricultural implements, cattle, etc., and the appropriation of the surplus product takes the form of the enserfed peasant working part of his time on his lord's land without compensation; in the bourgeois society the principal form of property is mobile capital, labour is free to move between capitalist producers and type of work, and the appropriation of the surplus product takes place through the market – labour power has become a commodity bought and sold in the market.

The economic and political power of the ruling class is reinforced by the ideology of that class, which constitutes the ruling ideas of society.

> The ideas of the ruling class are in every epoch the ruling ideas: i.e., the class which is the ruling material force of society is at the same time its ruling intellectual force. The class which has the means of production at its disposal, consequently also controls the means of mental production, so that the ideas of those who lack the means of mental production are on the whole subject to it.[23]

The Internal 'Law' of Historical Development, or the Transitions Between Modes of Production

It is in *The German Ideology* that for the first time we find a clear statement of the 'law' of historical development, the centre-piece of the new conception and the integration of all the various elements of this conception that Marx had worked out up to this point (1845).

> It is a fundamental condition of historical development that relations of production adapt to changes in the economy. By and large, this adaptation is maintained over long periods, even centuries. For example, the guild system of production successfully developed over a long period of time within the feudal mode of production; in fact, it became part of the feudal system. There was expansion of trade and accumulation of capital in the hands of merchants and money-lenders. Overall there were significant economic changes and new economic interests developed but they were within the frame of feudal relations.

But, and this is a crucial assumption, there comes a time in the course of development when relations of production fail to adapt to technical and economic changes. Marx wrote:

> In the development of productive forces there comes a stage when productive forces and means of intercourse [relations of production] are brought into being which, under the existing relations, only cause mischief, and are no longer productive, but destructive forces.[24]

This happens because the dominant class finds that the changes required in relations of production for progress to continue threaten its economic and social power. In this situation the existing relations become 'fetters' on further economic progress. To take an illustration: the feudal institution of serfdom (a particular form of feudal property) imposed serious 'fetters' on the development of the economy and capitalism, which required free mobility of labour.

In the letter to Annenkov, Marx wrote:

> Men never relinquish what they have won, but this does not mean that they never relinquish the social form in which they have acquired certain productive forces. On the contrary, in order that they may not be deprived of the result attained, and forfeit the fruits of civilisation, they are obliged, from the moment when the form of economic commerce [relations of production] no longer corresponds to the productive forces acquired, to change all their traditional social forms.[25]

But must there be forces that would remove the 'fetters' and restore the correspondence between the new forces of production and relations of production; why must historical progress be necessarily maintained?

We have here another of Marx's critical assumptions. The process of development itself generates forces that ensure that the required changes take place. The logic of this self-evolving, self-sustaining movement is neatly illustrated by Marx in the course of his discussion (in *Capital*) of technological development (under capitalism). He is here answering the question as to why technical and economic progress is not thwarted as a result of some internally created 'fetters'.

> There were mules and steam-engines before there were any workers exclusively occupied in making mules and steam-engines, in the same way as men wore clothes before there were any tailors. However, the inventions of Vauconson, Arkwright, Watt and others could be put into practice only because each inventor found a considerable number of skilled mechanical workers available, placed at their disposal by the period of manufacture.[26] Some of these workers were independent handicraftsmen of various trades, others were grouped together in

manufactures, in which, as we mentioned before, a division of labour of particular strictness prevailed. As inventions increased in number, and the demand for the newly discovered machines grew larger, the machine-making industry increasingly split up into numerous branches, and the division of labour within these manufactures developed accordingly. Here, therefore in manufacture, we see the immediate technical foundation of large-scale industry.[27]

The point here is that economic process is organic and evolutionary. The problems that arise in the course of economic and technological development are internal to the system and their solution and the requirements of progress are not unrelated to the resources that the process itself has generated; technical progress is not thwarted because the resources needed to give effect to it are not available. In general, the process of technological development does not present problems that society is unable to resolve.

It is this logic that Marx applies to historical development, that is, the transition from one mode of production to the next.

Marx's theory of the transition from capitalism to communism will be discussed at some length in the following chapter. Here only the general idea regarding the transition from one mode of production to the next mode is presented.

The process of development that creates the imbalance between the forces of production and relations of production also produces a class whose interest is tied up with the expansion of the new forces of production. It is this class, whose interests are aligned with the new forces of production that fights for appropriate changes in the institutions that facilitate economic expansion. Its adversary is, of course, the dominant class which has a vested interest in the existing relations of production. The battle takes place in the realm of politics and ideology – the emerging class must capture the machinery of the state to introduce the changes required for further development. The emerging class, associated as it with the forces of progress, is able to project its own interest as the general interest of society; it can claim to speak for the society as a whole. The success of this class signifies the transition from the old to the new mode of production. The transition may be achieved through a revolution or, in certain circumstances, by peaceful means.

In discussing these transitions, Marx often referred to the English bourgeois revolutions of the 17th century and the 1789 Revolution in France – revolutions that sealed the transition from feudalism to capitalism. Such social eruptions do no more than ratify the changes that have already taken place in society.

Here two points need particular emphasis. First, a social order cannot be displaced by a new one as long as relations of production continue to adapt to the requirements of production; that is, as long as the existing mode of production continues to deliver economic progress. It is only when its institutions become 'fetters' on further progress that it can be overthrown. Marx made this point clearly when in 1859 he wrote:

> No social order ever perishes before all the productive forces for which there is room in it have developed; and new higher relations of production [new social order] never appear before the material conditions of their existence have matured in the womb of the old society itself.[28]

Second, since the process of development is organic and evolutionary, the new social order can only grow out of the preceding one, a point made in the second part of the statement quoted above. This means that there are necessary stages in the process of development, that is, there are no leaps across social orders, say, from the feudal society to socialism. Bourgeois form of production is a necessary intermediate stage between the two, because it is this form of production that lays the material basis for socialism. It was noted in the preceding chapter that during the revolution of 1848-49 in Germany, Marx and his communist friends fought for the success of the bourgeois revolution, and when the big bourgeoisie failed to provide effective leadership, the communists' aim was to complete such a revolution working in collaboration with progressive elements in the bourgeoisie, the petty-bourgeoisie, peasants, etc. A new social order can only be achieved on the basis of the material conditions created by its predecessor. This idea is expressed a number of times in *The German Ideology*. For instance,

> Nor shall we explain to them [German philosophers] that it is possible to achieve real liberation only in the real world and by real means, that slavery cannot be abolished without the steam-engine and the mule jenny, serfdom cannot be abolished without improved agriculture, and that, in general, people cannot be liberated as long as they are unable to obtain food and drink, housing and clothing in adequate quality and quantity. 'Liberation' is a historical and not a mental act, and it is brought about by historical conditions, the [level] of industry, com[merce], agri[culture], [intercourse] then subsequently, in accordance with the definite stages of their development...[29]

International Dimension of the Materialist Conception

Up to this point our discussion has been based on the assumption that we are considering a closed society, a society that is completely isolated from the rest of the world. Such an assumption is necessary to understand the internal workings of a society, the so-called 'laws' of its development. But when we wish to understand its actual, historical experience it is necessary to move away from that assumption.

In fact, the international aspect of historical development looms large in Marx's discussion of the materialist conception. No country's development is isolated from what goes on in rest of the world. At the very beginning of the exposition of the materialist conception in *The German Ideology*, this point is made in clear terms:

> The relations of different nations among themselves depend upon the extent to which each has developed its productive forces, the division of labour and internal intercourse. This proposition is generally recognised. But not only the relations of one nation to others, but also the whole internal structure of the nation itself depends on the stage of development reached by its production and its internal and external intercourse.[30]

It is, of course, the development of capitalism that provides the main focus of Marx's work, and it is here that the international factor assumes its full significance in historical development. It is with the development of capitalism, from, say, 1500, that (as *The Communist Manifesto* put it) the 'natural exclusiveness of nations' was destroyed and development in different parts of the world made 'interdependent'. The development of capitalism itself was an international phenomenon (rather than entirely an internal process), a point which received particular emphasis:

> Manufacture and the movement of production in general received an enormous impetus through the extension of intercourse which came with the discovery of America and the sea-route to the East Indies. The new products imported thence, particularly the masses of gold and silver which came into circulation, had totally changed the position of the classes towards one another, dealing a hard blow to feudal landed property and to the workers; the expeditions of adventurers, colonisation, and above all the extension of markets into a world market, which had now become possible and was daily becoming more and more a fact, called forth a new phase of historical development...

> The expansion of commerce and manufacture accelerated the accumulation of movable capital, while in the guilds, which were not stimulated to extend their production, natural capital[31] remained stationary or even declined. Commerce and

manufacture created the big bourgeoisie; in the guild was concentrated the petty bourgeoisie.[32]

In the particular case of England, according to Marx, with the expansion of commerce and colonisation, the world demand for English manufactures could no longer be met by the industrial productive forces hitherto existing.

> This demand, outgrowing the productive forces, was the motive which, by producing large-scale industry – the application of elemental forces to industrial ends, machinery and the most extensive division of labour – called into existence the third period of property since the Middle Ages.[33]

Equally interesting is the fact that the development of capitalism in Europe since the end of the 15th century, as noted, had made development in different parts of the world interdependent. This idea crops up again and again both in Marx's theoretical discussions and in his commentaries on contemporary events. It appears a number of times in the first systematic account of the new conception, is repeated with great force in *The Communist Manifesto* and then appears in his writings during and immediately after the revolutions of 1848-49.

For instance, referring to the contradiction between the existing productive forces and the relations of production and the superstructure, Marx wrote:

> ... moreover, in a particular national sphere of relations this [contradiction] can also occur through the contradiction, arising not within the national orbit, but between this national consciousness and the practice of other nations, i.e., between the national and the general consciousness of a nation (as is happening now in Germany).[34]

A little later in the same volume (pp.74-75), he repeats this idea:

> Thus all collisions in history have their origin, according to our view, in the contradiction between the productive forces and the form of intercourse. Incidentally, to lead to a collision in a country, this contradiction need not necessarily have reached this extreme limit in that particular country. The competition with industrially more advanced countries, brought about by the expansion of international intercourse, is sufficient to produce a similar contradiction in countries with a less advanced industry (e.g., the latent proletariat in Germany brought into more prominence by the competition of English industry.)

He expressed the same idea 27 years later, in the Afterword to the second edition of the first volume of *Capital*.

We reach an important conclusion: given the openness of societies, the possibilities for social change or revolutions do not entirely depend on the material conditions prevailing in these societies taken individually and when international influences are neglected; the strict relationship between the economic base and superstructure is broken, or at least weakened, when relations with other countries are considered. These questions will be further discussed in the next chapter.

Role of the Conscious Human Agency in the Process of Development

The question of the relationship between the base and the superstructure has been referred to as the core of the 'Marx problem'. The discussion that follows explores this question.

It needs to be pointed out that the issue here is not whether forces of production – 'economic facts' – cause ideas to arise. (This point has already been discussed: for Marx production forces are not external to human consciousness, the distinction is simply that with respect to forces of production and the superstructure the same human consciousness is directed at different purposes.)

According to Marx the process of historical development is a 'spontaneous' process, that is, it is 'not subordinated to a general plan'. The question to be discussed here is the extent to which the conscious human agency (a government, a political party, an individual) can intervene in this process so that the actual course of development would be different from what it would have been without such intervention.

We start with the notion of the correspondence between conditions of production, relations of production and elements of the superstructure, such as ideology and belief systems, politics, etc.

Does this notion mean that at any given time we will expect to see complete and direct correspondence between them? If the answer is in the affirmative then Marx would have had to make the further assumption that there would be instantaneous adaptation of the elements of the superstructure to changing conditions of production and relations of production. That would be an extreme and preposterous assumption to make, and Marx certainly did not make it.

This means that we have to accept that there will always be a time lag between the changing material conditions and adaptation of the elements of the superstructure to these conditions. Some elements will adapt more readily, others will resist change. In other words, at any given time we will expect ideas, belief systems, traditions, etc., appropriate to an earlier mode of production to linger on in the successor mode and, therefore, exert a degree of impact on its working.

Though Marx did not discuss the question of the time lag directly, he was clearly aware of it, as is shown by the following passage in *The German Ideology* (where he is discussing the process of development as it actually proceeds over time):

> Since this development takes place spontaneously, i.e., is not subordinated to a general plan of freely combined individuals, it proceeds from various localities, tribes, nations, branches of labour, etc., each of which to start with develops independently of the others and only gradually enters into relations with the others. Furthermore, this development proceeds only very slowly; the various stages and interests are never completely overcome, but only subordinated to the prevailing interest and trail along beside the latter for centuries afterwards. It follows from this that even within a nation the individuals, even apart from their pecuniary circumstances, have quite diverse developments, and that an earlier interest, the peculiar form of intercourse of which has already been ousted by that belonging to a later interest, remains for a long time afterwards in possession of a traditional power in the illusory community (state, law), which has won an existence independent of the individuals.[35]

It will also be the case that at any given time we will find individuals whose thinking goes beyond the existing materials conditions. Again to quote from *The German Ideology* (where Marx is referring to colonies such as North America):

> ... they begin with the most advanced individuals of the old countries, and, therefore, with the correspondingly most advanced form of intercourse, even before this form of intercourse has been able to establish itself in the old countries.

And it is further remarked that

> consciousness can sometimes appear further advanced than contemporary conditions, so that in the struggle of a later epoch one can refer to earlier theoreticians as authorities.[36]

At a more practical level (as noted earlier), this disjunction is reinforced when we consider an open society, one that is open to the ideas and practices of other countries (which is of course the general case). As noted, Marx remarked on this consideration a number of times. Because of the historical struggles which took place in France and England, the 'theoretical awareness' of the German working class was much more advanced (in relation to conditions of production then prevailing in Germany) than would have been the case in the absence of access to the ideas of more advanced countries.

Let us now summarise. When we consider strict correspondence between the elements of the superstructure and conditions of production and relations of production we are thinking of a situation where all the adjustments in the former have been made in response to changes in the latter. Such a situation is an abstraction, a purely theoretical concept, not an actual historical situation. In the real world where change is always taking place (we are not considering a stagnating society) there will always be a time lag between changes in material conditions and those in the realm of ideas, belief systems, etc.

Ideas and practices of an earlier epoch will continue to battle with the new, progressive ideas of the new epoch and would eventually (and this may in some cases take a very long time) be completely superseded by the latter. Thus the old ideas may in such cases be said to have a degree of independence of the current material conditions. Further, there are individuals and groups – 'theoreticians' – whose thinking goes beyond the current empirical conditions, who can foresee, on the basis of certain existing tendencies, future developments, who can formulate ideals that can only be realised in the future. Add to these the ideas received from other nations which are more advanced in relation to current empirical conditions. All these ideas may be said to have a degree of independence of the existing material conditions. But these ideas are not hanging in the air. They arise out of the material conditions of the past and the present, and they interact with these conditions.

Let us now move to another aspect of the question being considered. Marx's first statement of the materialist conception (*The German Ideology*) suggested the role of the conscious human agency and the scope for intervention in the process of development. As noted earlier, Marx's exposition starts with the proposition according to which each generation receives from the preceding generation material conditions, a certain social structure, ideas, belief-systems, etc., acts on this inheritance, and 'on the one hand, continues the traditional activities in completely changed circumstances, and on the other, modifies the old circumstances with a changed activity'.

Marx put this idea more clearly in his letter to Annenkov. He wrote:

> It is superfluous to add that men are not free arbiters of their productive forces – which are the basis of all their history – for every productive force is an acquired force, the product of former activity. The productive forces are, therefore, the result of practical human energy; but this energy is itself circumscribed by the conditions in which men find themselves, by the productive forces already acquired, by the social form which exists

> before they do, which they do not create, which is the product of the preceding generation. Because of the simple fact that every succeeding generation finds itself in possession of the productive forces acquired by the preceding generation, which serves it as the raw material for new production, a coherence arises in human history, there is formed a history of humanity which is all the more a history of humanity since the productive forces of man and, therefore, his social relations have become more developed.[37]

Men are circumscribed, restricted by the fact that they are the product of circumstances, social forms, created before they appeared on the scene; it is this inheritance that has shaped their culture, attitudes and choosing preferences and mentalities. In this sense they are not free to choose. Further, the range of possibilities open to them is limited by this inheritance. For instance, those living in the technological environment of the hand-mill cannot suddenly make a leap to the world of the steam-mill because the raw material for such a transformation is not there. There is process of development that has necessarily to be gone through before this transition can be made. Similarly, those living in a tribal society cannot suddenly adopt West European democratic forms; they too must go through a necessary process of development before they can successfully adopt European institutions. The conscious human agency has freedom which is subject to both subjective and objective limitations: its choosing mentalities and the nature of the raw material available on which it can work. The future is not predetermined; conscious human agency can shape the inherited raw material but within certain limitations.

We see that on the objective side we have various, though in limited number of, possibilities, the raw material can be given only certain kinds of shape; on the subjective side we have the conscious human agency which can choose to adopt one course of action rather than another. Which of the available possibilities will be chosen?

At this point we have to recognise the fact that the human agency is not monolithic; it consists of different individuals, groups – 'theoreticians' – with different assessments of the prevailing situation and different views on the most effective course of action to be taken. For instance, one group of individuals may believe that the situation is ripe for a revolutionary uprising, another may take the opposite view. A revolution may fail simply because the leadership was not up to the task; at another time, the leadership may act prematurely. The future is not predetermined; it is not known; what shape it actually takes depends, at least in part, on the conscious human agency.

One particular aspect of this relationship has been the subject of much debate, that is the relationship between the state (the realm of politics) and the class structure of society. In the following paragraphs an attempt is made to briefly suggest some aspects of Marx's thinking on this question.

According to *The German Ideology* the modern state 'is nothing more than the form of organisation which the bourgeoisie are compelled to adopt, both for internal and external purposes, for the mutual guarantee of their property and interests.'[38] The same idea is expressed more dramatically in *The Communist Manifesto*: 'The executive of the modern state is but a committee for managing the common affairs of the whole bourgeoisie.'[39] These statements are in line with the materialist conception as, for instance, stated in the 1859 preface. It is in this sense that the state is dependent on (or not independent of) the social structure of society.

In apparent contrast with this idea, in *The Eighteenth Brumaire of Louis Bonaparte*, written three years after *The Manifesto*, Marx observed that 'under the second Bonaparte does the state seem to have made itself completely independent [of the class structure of society].'[40] This statement has led to the view that this notion of the state does not conform to the materialist conception and thus there is a discrepancy between the two.

In the same passage in *The German Ideology* where Marx expressed the view that the modern state is nothing but an organisation to defend bourgeois interests, Marx also observed that there are situations where the state does become independent of civil society. He wrote:

> The independence of the state is found nowadays in those countries where the [feudal] estates have not yet completely developed into classes, where the estates, done away with in more advanced countries, still play a part and exists a mixture, where consequently no section of the population can achieve dominance over the other. This is the case particularly in Germany.[41]

Marx repeated this idea in another part of *The German Ideology*.

> The bourgeoisie of little Holland, with its well-developed class interests, was more powerful than the far more numerous German middle class with its indifference and its divided petty interests. The fragmentation of interests was matched by the fragmentation of political organisation, the division into small principalities and free imperial cities. How could political concentration arise in a country which lacked all the economic conditions for it? The importance of each separate sphere of life (one can speak here neither of estates, nor of classes, but at most of former estates and classes not yet born) did not allow any one of them to gain exclusive domination. The inevitable consequence was that during the epoch of absolute monarchy,

which assumed here [Germany] its most stunted, semi-patri-archal form, the special sphere which, owing to division of labour, was responsible for the administration of public interests acquired an abnormal independence, which became still greater in the bureaucracy of modern times. Thus, the state built itself up into an apparently independent force, and this position, which in other countries was only transitory – a transition stage – it has maintained in Germany until the present day.[42]

Marx's *The Eighteenth Brumaire of Louis Bonaparte*, a short book of about hundred pages, is devoted to a discussion of events in France following the revolution of 1848, with a particular focus on the coup d'état of Louis Bonaparte (nephew of Napoleon Bonaparte). Louis Bonaparte was elected president of France, largely on peasant votes, on 10 December, 1848. Three years later, on 2 December, he mounted a coup, declared himself dictator and dispersed the national assembly. (A year later, he declared himself emperor.) Marx wrote *The Brumaire* immediately after the coup, over the months from December 1851 to March 1852.

Only under the second Bonaparte does the state seem to have made itself completely independent. As against civil society, the state machine has consolidated its position so thoroughly that the chief of the Society of December 10 suffices for its head, an adventurer blown in from abroad, raised on the shield by a drunken soldiery, which he had bought with liquor and sausages...[43]

Marx traces in detail the struggles of the various factions within the bourgeoisie. It was essentially because of these factional struggles that the bourgeoisie had become incapable of directly ruling the country, that is, through parliamentary means. Louis Bonaparte was able to seize power from direct bourgeois rule, but in substance the dictatorship defended bourgeois property and bourgeois conditions of production. Capitalism continued to flourish under Bonaparte's rule. It was the only form of class rule (given the backwardness of the peasantry, and the weakness of the working class) that was possible in the circumstances.

Writing 17 years later, this is how Marx distinguished his own analysis of Bonaparte's coup from the views of two contemporary writers:

Of the writings dealing with the same subject approximately at the same time as mine, only two deserve notice: Victor Hugo's *Napoleon the Little* and Proudhon's *Coup d'Etat*.

Victor Hugo confines himself to bitter and witty invective against the responsible publisher of the coup d'etat. The event itself appears in his work like a bolt from the blue. He sees in it only the violent act of a single individual. He does not notice that he makes the individual great instead of little by ascribing to him a personal power of initiative such as would be without parallel in world history. Proudhon, for his part, seeks to represent the coup d'etat as the result of an antecedent historical development. Unnoticeably, however, his historical construction of the coup d'etat becomes a historical apologia for its hero. Thus he falls into the error of our so-called objective historians. I, on the contrary, demonstrate how the class struggle in France created circumstances and relationships that made it possible for a grotesque mediocrity to play a hero's part.[44]

Marx clearly did not think that there was any discrepancy between his explanation of the 'independence' of the state under Louis Bonaparte (and in other historical situations) and his materialist conception.

We conclude that this is the only way to understand Marx's materialist conception. It is not meant to be a description of the world, nor a 'scientific law' but a guide to interpret the world. That is how Marx used it.

NOTES

1 *MECW* 5:38-39.
2 Ibid. p.3.
3 H. Allen Orr, 'Awaiting a new Darwin', the *New York Review of Books*, 7 February 2013.
4 See section 'Adam Smith as the Martin Luther of Political Economy.'
5 *MECW*, 5:40.
6 Ibid. p.37.
7 Preface to A Contribution to the Critique of Political Economy, *MESW*, 1:364.
8 *MESW*, vol. 2, pp.441-452.
9 *MECW*, 6:162.
10 *MESW*, 1:362.
11 Karl Marx, *Capital – Critique of Political Economy*, vol. 1, Penguin Books, London, 1990. p.100.
12 Teodor Shanin, *Late Marx and the Russian Road: Marx and the Peripheries of Capitalism*, Routledge & Kegan Paul, 1983, London, p.136.
13 Ibid. p.124.
14 *MECW*, 5:34.
15 Ibid. p.:50.
16 *MESW*, 2:242.
17 *MESW*, 1:362-63
18 *MECW*, 5: 36-37.
19 *MECW*, 5:42.
20 Ibid. p.54.
21 For instance, Joseph Schumpeter adopts the materialist approach, which he calls the 'economic interpretation of history', in his theory of development in which the central character in economic development is the entrepreneur or the innovator considered as an endogenous, economic factor. See his *The Theory of Economic Development*, Harvard University Press, Cambridge, MA, 1955, and *Capitalism, Socialism and Democracy*, Routledge, London, 1950.
22 *MESW*, 2: 452.
23 *MECW*, 5:59.
24 Ibid. p.52.
25 *MESW*, 2:443.
26 The 'manufacturing' period was one that preceded large-scale modern factory production. The 'manufacturing' system was a form of capitalist production, based on the handicraft technology perfected by the guild system, but practising division of labour.
27 *Capital*, vol. 1:503-04.
28 *MESW*, 1:363.
29 *MECW*, 5:38, see also p.54.
30 Ibid. p.32.

31 Natural capital is that which is tied to the person of the producer and his trade, as in the case of an artisan; movable or mobile capital is that which can be easily moved across industries and countries.

32 Ibid. pp.69-70.

33 Ibid. p.72.

34 Ibid. p.45.

35 Ibid. p.83

36 Ibid.

37 *MESW*, 2:442-43.

38 *MECW*, 5:90.

39 *MESW*, 1:36.

40 Ibid. p.333.

41 *MECW*, 5:90.

42 Ibid. 194-95.

43 *MESW*, 1:333.

44 Marx's preface to the second edition of *The Eighteenth Brumaire of Louis Bonaparte*, *MESW*, 1:242-43.

7

The Materialist Conception of History II:

The March into Communism

Preconditions for a Successful Revolution

As already noted the idea that development proceeds by stages means that one stage lays the material basis for the one that follows, and that means that for a new mode of production to come into existence certain definite conditions must be satisfied.

The first condition for the communist mode of production to come into being is that productive forces under capitalism must have developed to the extent that it produces an abundance of material goods. Communism cannot be established in a poor country. As *The German Ideology* put it:

> ...this development of productive forces ... is an absolutely necessary practical premise, because without it privation, *want* is merely made more general, and with *want* the struggle for necessities would begin again, and all the old filthy business would necessarily be restored.'[1]

There is enough material in *The Communist Manifesto* to show that Marx believed that the productive forces under capitalism in the advanced countries, such as Britain, had already reached that stage of development. At least there was the potential for the production of material goods in volumes that could provide the material basis for socialism. For instance:

> The bourgeoisie, during its rule of scarce one hundred years, has created more massive and more colossal productive forces than have all preceding generations together. Subjection of

Nature's forces to man, machinery, application of chemistry to industry and agriculture, steam navigation, railways, electric telegraph, clearing of whole continents for cultivation, canalisation of rivers, whole populations conjured out of the ground – what earlier century had even a presentiment that such productive forces existed in the lap of social labour.[2]

The second condition is that capitalism as a mode of production must have exhausted all its potential for further development; that is, its institutions relating to property, etc., were no longer able to adapt to changing conditions of production. To repeat what Marx wrote in 1859: no social order perishes before all the productive forces for which there is room in it have fully developed.

Here again, Marx thought that the point where capitalism had exhausted its potential for further development had already been reached in countries such as England or it was fast approaching that point.

The core of Marx's argument on this point as first developed in *The Communist Manifesto* may be expressed as follows: the central contradiction in capitalist production is that wages of labour are costs of production which must be kept as low as possible to realise high profits (which are necessary for expansion); at the same time to achieve high profits requires that there be sufficiently high level of effective demand in the economy for commodities to be sold at prices that would yield high profits; but the purchasing power from wages is insufficient to provide that level of effective demand. Hence the periodic occurrence of crises of over-production. Marx thought that in time these crises would become more and more acute, reflecting the increasing weakness of the system.[3] To quote again from *The Communist Manifesto*:

Productive forces at the disposal of society no longer tend to further the development of the conditions of bourgeois property; on the contrary, they have become too powerful for these conditions, by which they are fettered... The conditions of bourgeois society are too narrow to comprise the wealth created by them.[4]

The conclusion is that private ownership of the means of production is now incompatible with the social character of production; the bourgeoisie has thus lost its earlier dynamic; it can no longer take the development process any further. It has become unfit to rule.

The demise of capitalist mode of production would not result in chaos. The process of development under capitalism has also created the forces that would take society forward. This aspect of the process relates to the situation and development of the proletariat. There are three points here.

First, capitalism is – has been – unable to improve the material conditions of workers. Also, because of the extensive use of machinery, work has lost its individual character, worker has become an appendage of the machine. Further, because of the standardised nature of work more and more women and children have been drawn into factory employment putting a downward pressure on wages that are pushed down to the level of subsistence.

Second, with the greater efficiency of machine-based production, handicraftsmen, small independent traders, etc., large sections of the middle class sink into the ranks of the proletariat. Society is increasingly polarised between the wealthy and the poor. Capitalist development 'renders the great mass of humanity propertyless, and this in contradiction to the world of wealth and culture.'[5] Marx was aware that there were tendencies in the working of capitalism operating in the opposite direction, but he assumed that the tendencies working for the polarisation of society would dominate.

The third point relates to the development of the proletariat's struggle with the bourgeoisie, a struggle whose progress runs parallel with the development of capitalism. In the early stages of this development, workers form an incoherent mass, scattered over the country. But with the development of industry, and particularly with increasing concentration of capital in large enterprises and concentration in certain localities, the labour force also gets consolidated, its interests and conditions of life become more and more equalised, and its class consciousness and strength grow. Numerous local struggles are centralised in one national struggle – between classes, the proletariat and the bourgeoisie. 'But every class struggle is a political struggle.' The conclusion arrived at is:

> In depicting the most general phases of the development of the proletariat, we traced the more or less veiled civil war raging within existing society, up to the point where that war breaks out into open revolution, and where the violent overthrow of the bourgeoisie lays the foundation for the sway of the proletariat.[6]

It should be added here that Marx recognised that there would be circumstances in which the transition from capitalism to socialism could be achieved by peaceful means. In his 1872 Amsterdam Speech he said that countries like England and Holland which had not been 'bureaucratised' had a good chance of a peaceful revolution.

However, the actual process of transition from capitalism to communism is complicated by what in the preceding chapter we referred to as the international dimension of the materialist conception. It is important to note that Marx's argument is not about the development of capitalism in one specific country; it is about capitalism as a mode of production, a mode which is a world-system. This idea is put clearly in *The German Ideology*: the general development of productive forces 'implies the actual empirical existence of men in their world-historical, instead of local being...'

> ... only with this universal development of productive forces is a *universal* intercourse between men established ... making each nation dependent on the revolutions of the others, and finally puts *world-historical*, empirically universal individuals in place of local ones. Without this, 1) communism could only exist as a local phenomenon; 2) the *forces* of intercourse themselves could not have developed as *universal*, hence unendurable powers; they would have remained home-bred 'conditions' surrounded by superstition; and 3) and each extension of intercourse would abolish local communism. Empirically, communism is only possible as the act of dominant peoples 'all at once' and simultaneously ...[7]

The Communist Manifesto which highlighted the worldwide scope of capitalism, referred to this point only briefly:

> Though not in substance, yet in form, the struggle of the proletariat with the bourgeoisie is at first national struggle. The proletariat of each country must, of course, first of all settle matters with its own bourgeoisie.

And it distinguished communists from other working class parties by this:

> 1. In the national struggles of the proletarians of the different countries, they point out and bring to the front the common interests of the entire proletariat, independently of all nationality. 2. In the various stages of development which the struggle of the working class against the bourgeoisie has to pass through, they always and everywhere represent the interests of the movement as a whole.[8]

As noted in Chapter 5 above, writing on the experience of the 1848-49 revolutions in Europe, Marx made a number of observations on this subject which included a very practical point, that is, a communist revolution in one country would be thwarted by a coalition of advanced capitalist countries. For this reason alone to be successful a revolution would have to take place around the same time at least in some of the most advanced and powerful countries.

There is another dimension of the international factor. When we move away from the assumption of a closed economy and society, we find that capital can move across national boundaries and find more profitable investment opportunities than those available in the national market, find cheaper raw materials and more profitable market for their products. In such circumstances the central contradiction of capitalism referred to earlier as the insufficiency of effective demand and pressure on the rate of profit is significantly eased or modified. Paradoxically, in such conditions Marx's vision of capitalism as a world, rather than a national, system is increasingly realised, and at the same time the analysis of the breakdown of capitalism and the prospects of a communist revolution become more problematic.[9]

The conclusion must be that the actual overthrowing of worldwide capitalism and the proletarian revolution would have to be a prolonged and complex process the precise shape of which could neither be theorised nor predicted.

After the Revolution

After a successful revolution and seizure of political power by the proletariat, there is a long transitional period – the first phase of communist society – during which the state can be 'nothing but the dictatorship of the proletariat'. The expression 'revolutionary dictatorship of the proletariat' is used by Marx in his 'Marginal Notes on the Programme of the German Workers' Party' (referred to as *Critique of the Gotha Programme*), written in 1875. This expression is not used in *The German Ideology*, nor in *The Communist Manifesto*. *The Manifesto* refers to the necessity ('in the beginning') of making 'despotic inroads on the rights of property, and on the conditions of bourgeois production.'[10] In *The Civil War in France* (1871), Marx applauded the constitution of the political authority established in the Paris Commune (a potential form for the first phase of communist society) which consisted of municipal councillors, 'chosen by universal suffrage and revocable at short terms'; and he noted that this was to be a working, not parliamentary, body, 'both executive and legislative at the same time'.[11]

It is obvious that in the wake of a successful proletarian revolution different forms of governmental power would be possible depending on the specific circumstances of every country. The central point in this context, as he put in *The Civil War in France*, is that the 'working class cannot simply lay hold of the ready-made state machinery, and wield it for its own purposes.'[12] Whatever forms the new arrangements took, they will have to crush the existing state power and set up new structures that would be capable of making effective inroads on bourgeois conditions of production.

During the first phase many of the features of bourgeois society will persist. In the *Critique of the Gotha Programme*, Marx wrote: 'What we have to deal with here is a communist society, not as it has developed on its own foundations, but, on the contrary, just as it *emerges* from the capitalist society; which is thus in every respect, economically, morally, intellectually, still stamped with the birth marks of the old society from whose womb it emerges.'[13]

It follows from this that the distribution of the national product among members of society will be governed by the same principles that govern income distribution under capitalism; this in the sense that the principle of distribution will recognise physical and mental differences between individuals; 'unequal' individuals will receive unequal rewards – 'to each according to his work'. This will mean that there will be a significant degree of inequality in society, depending on education, skills, intensity of labour, etc. 'Right can never be higher than the economic structure of society and its cultural development conditioned thereby.'[14]

In order to change bourgeois conditions of production during this phase the proletariat will

> wrest by degrees all capital from the bourgeoisie, centralise all instruments of production in the hands of the state, which has now become the proletariat organised as political power, and to increase the total of productive forces as rapidly as possible.[15]

During this phase we still have wage labour; the difference with the capitalist system is that all are employed by society or the state. The surplus product is used for investment to expand productive forces, and for social purposes, including the improvement of the standard of living of the people.

The Manifesto proposed a number of measures that the proletariat will undertake to start with. It noted that these measures will apply differently in different countries, depending on their specific circumstances. The preface to the 1872 edition of The Manifesto noted that no special stress was laid on these measures and added that that passage would, in every respect, be very differently worded today.

The measures proposed are: Abolition of property in land and application of all rents of land to public purposes; a heavy progressive tax on income; abolition of all right of inheritance; confiscation of all property of emigrants and rebels; centralisation of credit in the hands of the state by means of a national bank; nationalisation of the means of communication and transport; extension of instruments of production owned by the state; equal liability of all to labour; establishment of industrial armies, especially for agriculture; gradual abolition of the distinction between town and country; free education; abolition of child labour in its present form; combination of education with industrial production.

The first phase of communist society is a long drawn process during which society has to be transformed and the foundations for the second phase are to be laid. The proletariat has to create mass scale communist consciousness, the 'muck of ages' has got to be rid of, and the roots of bourgeois society uprooted and destroyed so that people in general become fitted to form the new society and acquire the faculty to govern themselves.[16] The first stage is essentially a transitory and preparatory stage.

Higher Stages of Communist Society

Marx made no attempt to give a systematic and unified account of the institutional structure of the second phase of communist society. What we have are fragmentary observations made on different occasions. In *The German Ideology* no particular distinction is made between the first and second stages though an important feature of the higher stage of the communist society is clearly outlined. It is in *The Communist Manifesto* that the distinction is clearly made for the first time. Here there is only one short passage on the second phase. There are further comments in *The Civil War in France* when he is discussing the suppression of the Paris Commune and there is a short paragraph in the *Critique of the Gotha Programme*.

Marx's circumspection with regard to any discussion of details about the features and the institutional frame of a higher phase of communist society is perhaps the result of his use of his own materialist method. As we have seen, according to this method future develops through tensions in the present-day society, and our understanding of the future depends on our understanding of the developing tendencies we observe today. It was thus possible to conceptualise, up to a point, the first phase of the communist society as it was 'emerging' from the 'womb' of contemporary capitalism. We can see that from the revolutionary measures to be adopted immediately after the revolution. But there was no material basis for conceptualising the institutional framework which would only materialise in the distant future and which at the present could exist only in the realm of consciousness. Marx could not have followed the utopian socialists, whom he had severely chastised for making blueprints for a future society.

However, despite being fragmentary his observations on the higher stages of the communist society do give us a reasonably good idea what he had in mind.

As we have seen (Chapters 1 and 3), it was in Marx's critique of Hegel's philosophy of law that the starting point of his discussion of the features of an ideal society was formed. The central issue here was the problem of dualism between civil society, the domain in which people make their living, and the political domain or the state which claims to serve the general interest of society. (We recall that the critique focused on Hegel's failure to resolve the problem.) Although in the course of the development of his thought Marx's language on the subject changed, the overcoming of the dichotomy between the private interest (civil society) and the general interest (the state) remained fundamental to his vision of the ideal society. The ideal society would be one that restores the integration of the individual with society – integration that had characterised pre-capitalist societies (their oppressive character notwithstanding) and that had been destroyed by the individualism of capitalism. As pointed out earlier, the idea of the future communist society was already present in 1843 when Marx was not yet a communist.

The notion of overcoming dualism between civil society and the political realm is founded on the premise that society and individual are not two distinct entities; one includes the other. There is no aspect of an individual's life which excludes society.

The first phase of communist society will prepare the ground for the resolution of the problem of dualism by fundamentally transforming the character of civil society and with it the character of public authority.

Although, as noted, no clear distinction between different phases of communism is made in *The German Ideology*, Marx here identifies one of the most significant features of the higher stage. In this stage man will make history *consciously* rather than *spontaneously* as has happened up to the present.

> This fixation of social activity, this consolidation of what we ourselves produce into a material power above us, growing out of our control, thwarting our expectations, bringing to naught our calculations, is one of the chief factors in historical development up till now. The social power, i.e., the multiplied productive force, which arises through the co-operation of different individuals as it is caused by the division of labour, appears to these individuals, since their cooperation is not voluntary but has come about naturally, not as their united power, but as an alien force existing outside them, of the origin and goal of which they are ignorant, which on the contrary passes through a peculiar series of phases and stages independent of the will and the action of man, nay even being the prime governor of these.'[17]

> Communism differs from all previous movements in that it overturns the basis of all earlier relations of production and intercourse, and for the first time consciously treats all naturally evolved premises as the creations of hitherto existing men, strips them of their natural character and subjugates them to the power of united individuals. Its organisation is, therefore, essentially economic, the material production of the conditions of this unity; it turns existing conditions into conditions of unity. The reality which communism creates is precisely the true basis for rendering it impossible that anything should exist independently of individuals insofar as reality is nevertheless only a product of the preceding intercourse of individuals.[18]

Instead of being driven by the blind forces of the market, future development will be socially, consciously planned.

The short paragraph in *The Communist Manifesto* makes the point that when during the first phase all class distinctions have disappeared and pro-

duction is concentrated in the hand of 'a vast association of the whole nation, the public power will lose its political character.' And, then in place of
the old bourgeois society, with its classes and class antagonisms, we shall
have an association, in which the free development of each is the condition
for free development of all.'[19]

There is a brief observation on the higher stage of communism in the
Gotha Programme:

> In a higher phase of communist society, after the enslav-
> ing subordination of the individual to the division of labour,
> and therewith also the antithesis between mental and physi-
> cal labour, has vanished; after labour has become not only the
> means of life but life's prime want; after the productive forces
> have also increased with the all-round development of the in-
> dividual, and all the springs of cooperative wealth flow more
> abundantly – only then can the narrow horizon of bourgeois
> right be crossed in its entirety and society inscribe on its ban-
> ners: From each according to his ability, to each according to
> his need.[20]

This paragraph follows the discussion of the principle of income distribution in the first phase of communist society, during which, as noted, each
individual producer receives back from society what he gives to it in the
form of his labour.

The closest Marx came to suggesting the outlines of the institutional
arrangements of the higher phase of communist society is to be found in
his *Civil War in France*. Marx suggests here what the Paris Commune could
have done had it been able to survive (even though he thought it could not
have survived; in fact, it was not socialist, nor could it have been.)[21] Marx
is clearly projecting his own thinking about what the higher phase of communist society should be like on to what the Paris Commune would have
done had it survived (and had it been socialist). We get here an idea of what
a society where the dualism between the political realm and civil society
has been overcome and therefore the state as we know it has been abolished
would look like. He wrote:

> The Paris Commune was, of course, to serve as a model to all
> the great industrial centres of France. The communal regime
> once established in Paris and the secondary centres, the old
> centralised Government would in the provinces, too, have to
> give way to the self-government of the producers. In a rough
> sketch of national organisation which the Commune had no
> time to develop, it states clearly that the Commune was to be
> the political form of the smallest country hamlet, and that in

the rural districts the standing army was to be replaced by a national militia, with an extremely short term of service. The rural communes of every district were to administer their common affairs by an assembly of delegates in the central town, and these district assemblies were again to send deputies to the National Delegation in Paris, each delegate to be at any time revocable and bound by the *mandate imperative* (formal instructions) of his constituents. The few but important functions which still would remain for a central government were not to be suppressed, as has been intentionally mis-stated, but were to be discharged by Communal, and therefore strictly responsible agents. The unity of the nation was not to be broken, but, on the contrary, to be organised by the Communal Constitution and to become a reality by the destruction of the State power which claimed to be the embodiment of that unity independent of, and superior to, the nation itself, from which it was a parasitic excrescence. While the merely repressive organs of the old governmental power were to be amputated, its legitimate functions were to be wrested from an authority usurping pre-eminence over society itself, and restored to the responsible agents of society. Instead of deciding once in three or six years which member of the ruling class was to misrepresent the people in Parliament, universal suffrage was to serve the people, constituted in Communes ...[22]

It is evident that Marx's ideal society is not ideal because it is able to provide its members greater and greater abundance of material goods, say, more and more and faster and faster cars. It is a remarkable fact that the question of the rising standard of living in material terms hardly ever appears in Marx's thinking about the nature of the communist society of the future. He simply took it for granted that in a developed communist society forces of production would become more and more powerful and its members would enjoy an improving standard of living. But this standard will consist of the creation and satisfaction of needs that are genuinely human, in contrast to capitalism that creates, and then satisfies, needs that are not always human. Marx would still be a communist even if he could have been persuaded that eventually capitalism would be able to provide the bulk of the population more and more material goods.

We conclude this discussion with the following moving passage that, we think, gives a good indication of Marx's deepest thought on the nature of the developed communist society. It comes from notes written in 1857-58, in preparation for his *Capital*.

Among the ancients we discover no single enquiry as to which form of landed property, etc., is the most productive, which creates maximum wealth. Wealth does not appear as the aim of production, although Cato may well investigate the most profitable cultivation of fields, or Brutus may even lend money at the most favourable rate of interest. The enquiry is always about what kind of property creates the best citizens...

Thus the ancient conception, in which man always appears (in however narrowly national, religious or political a definition) as the aim of production, seems very much more exalted than the modern world, in which production is the aim of man and wealth is the aim of production. In fact, however, when the narrow bourgeois form has been peeled away, what is wealth if not the universality of needs, capacities, enjoyments, productive powers, etc., of individuals, produced in universal exchange? What, if not the full development of human control over the forces of nature – those of his own nature as well as those of so-called 'nature'? What, if not the absolute elaboration of his creative dispositions? ... In the bourgeois political economy – and in the epoch of production to which it corresponds – this complete elaboration of what lies within man, appears as the total alienation, and the destruction of all fixed, one-sided purposes as the sacrifice of the end in itself to a wholly external compulsion. Hence in one way the childlike world of the ancients appears to be superior; and this is so, in so far as we seek for closed shape, form and established limitation. The ancients provide a narrow satisfaction, whereas the modern world leaves us unsatisfied, or, where it appears to be satisfied with itself is *vulgar* and *mean*.[23]

NOTES

1 *MECW*, 5:49.
2 *MESW*, 1:39.
3 I need to point out that this statement is a highly simplified account of Marx's observations on capitalist crises.
4 Ibid. pp. 39-40.
5 *MECW*, 5:48.
6 *MESW*, 1:45.
7 *MECW*, 5:49.
8 *MESW*, 1:45, 46.
9 Lenin's *Imperialism: the Highest Stage of Capitalism* deals with some of these issues.
10 *MESW*, 1: p.53.
11 *MESW*, 1: 519.
12 Ibid.
13 *MESW*, 2:23.
14 Ibid. p.24.
15 *MESW*, 1:53.
16 *MECW*, 5:52-53.
17 Ibid. p.47-48.
18 Ibid. p.81.
19 *MESW*, 1:54.
20 *MESW*, 2:24
21 Letter to Ferdinand Domela-Nieuwenhuis, dated 22 February 1881. *Marx-Engels Selected Correspondence*, International Publishers, New York, 1968.
22 *MESW*, 1:520.
23 *Grundrisse – Foundations of the Critique of Political Economy* (Rough draft), translated with a foreword by Martin Nicolaus, Penguin Books, London, 1973, pp.487-88. The translation given here is from *Karl Marx: Pre-Capitalist Economic Formations*, translated by Jack Cohen and edited by E. J. Hobsbawm, Lawrence and Wishart, London, 1964, pp. 84-85.

8

Epilogue

The worldview as presented in the preceding chapters provided the foundation on which Marx would develop his own theory of political economy. Within months of the completion of *The German Ideology* (1846), he clearly stated his main critique of the classical political economy of Adam Smith and David Ricardo. He wrote:

> He [Proudhon] has not observed that economic categories are only the abstractions of these real relations [of production], and that they are valid as long as these conditions exit. Hence he commits the error of bourgeois economists who consider these economic categories to be eternal laws and not historical laws which remain laws only during a certain historical development determined by productive forces.[1]

Less than a year later he elaborated this observation in his *Poverty of Philosophy*, which he said (in 1880) contained 'in embryo what after a labour of twenty years became the theory that was developed in *Capital*.'[2]

The point here is not that classical political economists lacked knowledge of history. Adam Smith had identified various stages in the development of human society and noted some important elements in the theory of development. But he had confined this development within the frame of capitalist relations. In his theory the economy developed to the point where too much capital had been accumulated so that the rate of profit had declined to the point where there was no further investment and no economic growth. The capitalist economy had reached its stationary state. That was the end of historical development. Similarly, Ricardo conceived economic development entirely within the frame of capitalist relations. His theory was aimed at generating policy which if adopted would stem the decline in the rate of profit and therefore in investment and economic growth.

Marx's critique of classical political economy at this point was directed at this idea of capitalist development. For classical political economists

> there has been history, but there is no longer any. There has been history, since there were the institutions of feudalism, and in these institutions of feudalism we find quite different relations of production from those of bourgeois society, which the economists try to pass off as natural and as such eternal.[3]

Marx's own theory of political economy, taking the classical theory as its starting point, sought to identify forces within the capitalist economy that would provide the dynamic of historical development, that is, changes in the capitalist mode of production. The fundamental point here is that the capitalist society, like all earlier societies based on the division of society between property owners and those who work for them, is based on antagonism. Adam Smith had noted the presence of class antagonism in capitalist society but had failed to follow it up. Ricardo had highlighted antagonism between the capitalist class and landowners, but had ignored that between capitalists and the working class. In Marx' critique of political economy the antagonism between the propertied owning class and the working class takes centre stage.

For instance, with the development of forces of production the economic structure of the capitalist society and with it relations of production themselves change – something completely missing in classical political economy. With the growth in forces of production, size of the typical business increases, there is increasing concentration of capital, and with it there is increase in the size and class consciousness of the working class. It is this antagonism that provides the dynamic of historical change.

In *The Poverty of Philosophy*, Marx wrote that just as political economists were the 'scientific representatives' of the bourgeoisie, so the communists were the 'theoreticians' of the working class. So long as the working class was not yet sufficiently developed in size and class consciousness utopian thinking prevailed. But with the development of the working class for communist theoreticians 'science, which is provided by the historical movement and associating itself consciously with it, has ceased to be doctrinaire and has become revolutionary.'[4]

This is the vision to which Marx's theory of political economy sought to give effect, to theoretically demonstrate the mechanism of transition from capitalism to communism.

NOTES

1 *Letters on 'Capital'*, p.11.
2 *MECW*, 6: xviii.
3 *MECW*, 6:176
4 *MECW*, 6:177-78.

Works Cited

Avineri, Shlomo, *The Social and Political Thought of Karl Marx*, Cambridge University Press, London, 1975.

Berlin, Isaiah, *Karl Marx His Life and Environment*, A Galaxy Book, Oxford University Press, New York, 1959.

Edgley, Roy, 'Dialectical Materialism' in John Eatwell, Murray Millgate and Peter Newman, eds., *The New Palgrave Marxian Economics*, Macmillan, London and Basingstoke, 1990.

Engels, Frederick, 'On the History of the Communist Party', *Marx Engels Selected Works* (*MESW*), vol.2, Foreign Languages Publishing House, Moscow, 1958.

       Socialism: Utopian and Scientific, *MESW*, vol. 2.

       Ludwig Feuerbach and the End of the Classical German Philosophy, *MESW*, vol. 2.

       'Outlines of a Critique of Political Economy', *Karl Marx Frederick Engels Collected Works* (*MECW*), vol. 3, Lawrence & Wishart, London, 1975.

Hegel, G. W. F., *Outlines of the Philosophy of Right* (translated by T. M. Knox), Oxford University Press, Oxford, 2008.

       The Philosophy of History, Dover Publications, New York, 1956.

Hobsbawm, E. J., ed., *Karl Marx – Pre Capitalist Formations* (translated by Jack Cohen), Lawrence & Wishart, London, 1964.

Mann, Golo, *The History of Germany Since 1789*, Penguin, Harmondsworth, 1974.

Marx, Karl, 'Letter to Father', *MECW*, vol. 1, 1975.

Doctoral Dissertation 'Difference Between Democritean and Epicurean Philosophy of Nature', *MECW*, vol. 1, 1975.

'Contribution to the Critique of Hegel's Philosophy of Law' (the *Hegel Critique*), *MECW*, vol. 3, 1975.

'On the Jewish Question', *MECW*, vol. 3, 1975.

'Contribution to the Critique of Hegel's Philosophy of Law: Introduction', *MECW*, vol. 3, 1975.

'Critical Marginal Notes on the Article 'The King of Prussia and Social Reform: By a Prussian'', *MECW*, vol. 3, 1975.

The Economic and Philosophical Manuscripts of 1844, *MECW*, vol. 3, 1975.

The Holy Family, or Critique of Critical Criticism (with Engels), *MECW*, vol. 4, 1975.

Theses on Feuerbach, *MECW*, vol. 5, 1976.

The German Ideology (with Engels), *MECW*, vol. 5, 1976.

'Letter to Annenkov', *MESW*, vol. 2, 1958.

The Poverty of Philosophy: Answer to the Philosophy of Poverty by M. Proudhon, *MECW*, vol. 6, 1976.

Manifesto of the Communist Party, *MESW*, vol. 1, 1958.

'The Bourgeoisie and the Counter Revolution in Vienna', *MECW*, vol. 7, 1977.

'The Crisis and the Counter Revolution', *MECW*, vol. 7, 1977.

'Counter Revolution in Berlin', *MECW*, vol. 8, 1977.

'The Revolutionary Movement', *MECW*, vol. 8, 1977.

'The Summary Suppression of the *Neue Rheinische Zeitung*, *MECW*, vol. 9, 1977.

'To the Workers of Cologne', *MECW*, vol. 9, 1977.

The Eighteenth Brumaire of Louis Bonaparte, *MESW*, vol. 1, 1958.

Grundrisse: Foundations of the Critique of Political Economy, Penguin Books, London, 1973.

Preface to *A Contribution to the Critique of Political Economy*, *MESW*, vol. 1, 1958.

Capital: A Critique of Political Economy, vol. 1, Penguin Books, London, 1976.

Preface to the second edition of *The Eighteenth Brumaire of Louis Bonaparte*, *MESW*, vol. 1, 1958.

The Civil War in France, *MESW*, vol. 1, 1958.

'Afterword' [Postface] to the second edition of *Capital*, vol. 1, Penguin Books, London, 1976.

'Marginal Notes to the Programme of the German Workers' Party' ['Critique of the Gotha Programme'], *MESW*, vol. 2, 1958.

'A letter to the Editorial Board of *Otechestvennye Zapiski*' in Teodor Shanin, *Late Marx and the 'Peripheries of Capitalism'*, Routledge &

Kegan Paul, London, 1983.

'Letter to Vera Zasulich' in *Letters on 'Capital by Karl Marx & Frederick Engels* (translated by Andrew Drummond), New Park Publications, London, 1983.

McLellan, David, *Karl Marx – His Life and Work*, Paladin, St. Albans, Herts., 1977.

Marx's Grundrisse, Paladin, St. Albans, Herts., 1973.

Mehring, F. *Karl Marx – The Story of His Life*, George Allen & Unwin, London, 1936.

Orr, H. Allen, 'Awaiting a New Darwin', *New York Review of Books*, 7 February 2013.

Rahim, Eric, 'Marx - From Hegel and Feuerbach to Adam Smith: A New Synthesis', *International Critical Thought*, vol. 8, issue 2, 2018.

Rigby, S. H., *Marxism and History – A Critical Introduction*, Manchester University Press, Manchester and New York, 1998.

Sabine, George and Thorson, Thomas, L., *A History of Political Theory*, 4th ed., Holt, Rinehart and Winston, Fort Worth, 1973.

Schumpeter, Joseph, *History of Economic Analysis*, George Allen & Unwin, London, 1954.

Capitalism, Socialism and Democracy, Routledge, London and New York, 1994.

Smith, Adam, *Theory of Moral Sentiments*, D. D. Raphael and A.L. Macfie, eds., Clarendon Press, Oxford, 1976.

An Inquiry into the Nature and Causes of the Wealth of Nations, R. H. Campbell and A. S. Skinner, eds., Clarendon Press, Oxford, 1976.

Sperber, Jonathan, *Karl Marx – A Nineteenth Century Life*, Liveright Publishing Corporation, New York, 2013.

Stedman Jones, Gareth, *Karl Marx – Greatness and Illusions*, Allen Lane, UK, 2016.

Tucker, Robert, C.. *Philosophy and Myth in Karl Marx*, Cambridge University Press, London, 1961.

Wheen, Francis, *Karl Marx*, Fourth Estate, London, 1999.

Index

About the author

ERIC RAHIM was born in 1928, in what was then still British-ruled India. Having graduated from Forman Christian College, Lahore, in 1948 he worked in the English-language newspaper *Dawn*, Karachi, and subsequently for *The Pakistan Times*, Lahore. In 1958 he left Pakistan to study economics in London.

He graduated from University College London (UCL) in 1961, obtaining a BSc. (Econ) degree with first-class honours, a later completed a (London) Ph.D. on Michal Kalecki's theory of income distribution. He was appointed in 1963 to a Lectureship, later to a Senior Lectureship, at Strathclyde University, Glasgow, Scotland,; currently, he is an Honorary Senior Lecturer.

Aside from his teaching career, focussing on economic theory and development economics, he has worked overseas in Ethiopia, Pakistan and Turkey on British Council and OECD programmes, and with the World Bank and United Nations Social and Economic Commission for Asia and the Pacific. He is the author of numerous articles in the academic press and progressive media.

A PROMETHEAN VISION IS PUBLISHED JOINTLY WITH THE MARX MEMORIAL LIBRARY

Marx Memorial Library & Workers' School was founded in 1933 with the aim of advancing education, knowledge and learning in all aspects of the science of Marxism, the history of Socialism and the working class movement.

At the heart of the British Labour Movement for over 80 years, the Library is home to a unique collection of published and archival sources on related subjects including the trade unionism, peace and solidarity movements and the Spanish Civil War.

The Library's education programme – online and onsite – examines subjects ranging from Marxist political economy to socialist art. The Library itself is a historic building rooted in Clerkenwell's radical tradition. We are a charity, financed by members and affiliates.

To join, donate or otherwise support the Library please contact
Marx Memorial Library & Workers' School
37a Clerkenwell Green, London EC1R 0DU

Tel: +44 207 253 1485
m.jump@marx-memorial-library.org.uk

www.marx-memorial-library.org.uk

ORDER PRAXIS PRESS TITLES

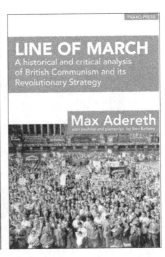

MARX200
The Significance of Marxism in the 21st Century
Leading scholars and activists from different countries – including Cuba, India and the UK – show that Marx's ideas continue to provide us with the analysis we need to understand our world today in order to change it.

1000 DAYS OF REVOLUTION
Chilean Communists on the lessons of Popular Unity 1970-73
A fascinating account of the Allende Presidency, the dilemmas of peaceful and armed struggle for socialism, the role of US imperialism and domestic right-wing forces, and a self critical evaluation of the role of Chilean communists.

HARDBOILED ACTIVIST by Ken Fuller
The work and politics of writer Dashiell Hammett, crime fiction legend, communist and staunch opponent of McCarthyism. A critical review of his work and a definitive account of his political stand.

WHITE COLLAR, RED TIES by Steve Parsons (forthcoming)
A unique study of the Communist Party of Great Britain's activities among professional workers and intellectuals from its foundation until 1956. An essential contribution to the history of the British left.

LINE OF MARCH by Max Adereth (forthcoming)
A new edition of Max Adereth's historical analysis of British communism, focusing on the development of the party's various programmes. First published 1994.

For more details, contact praxispress@me.com

BUY online, with free shipping, at www.redletterspp.com

CPSIA information can be obtained
at www.ICGtesting.com
Printed in the USA
LVHW051654190421
684911LV00011B/1546

9 781899 155088